W9-BVJ-502

HOW TO BE HAPPY THOUGH MARRIED

by Tim LaHaye

Tyndale House Publishers
Wheaton, Illinois

How to Be Happy Though Married

Copyright © 1968, Tyndale House Publishers,
Wheaton, Illinois. All rights reserved.

Twenty-eighth printing, September 1979
Over 600, 000 copies in print

Library of Congress Card Number: 68-31703
ISBN 8423-1500-4, Cloth
ISBN 8423-1501-2, Paper

Drawings by Jean Redmond.

Printed in United States of America.

OVERTON MEMORIAL LIBRARY
HERITAGE CHRISTIAN UNIVERSITY
P.O. Box HCU
Florence, Alabama 35630

CONTENTS

Foreword 5

Introduction 7

1 / OPPOSITES ATTRACT 11

2 / FORGET YOURSELF 25

3 / SPIRITUAL ADJUSTMENT 41

4 / PHYSICAL JOYS 53

5 / ADJUSTING TO CHILDREN 75

6 / SIX KEYS TO MARITAL HAPPINESS 97

Appendix A: The Spirit-filled Person 129

Appendix B: From My Counseling File 143

This book is lovingly dedicated

to my wife, Beverly.

Her patient understanding and loving tenderness

have made our marriage an increasingly

joyous experience. Her inner beauty,

"the hidden woman of the heart,"

like her physical beauty,

has improved through these twenty years.

Every day I thank God for bringing

her into my life.

From the Private Library of
P. Craig Collins

FOREWORD

How can two Christians unite to form one spiritual, emotional, and physical body through marriage? This vital question is openly discussed by Pastor LaHaye in a unique manner. Drawing on years of experience in counseling and a gift for understanding the human personality, Pastor LaHaye describes the joys of marriage, diagnoses the major potential problems, disects causes of incompatability and directs the reader to practical spiritual solutions. The discussion of six keys to marital happiness (maturity, submission, love, communication, prayer and Christ) should be helpful to those far along the path of matrimony as well as those just taking their first steps together. Unlike many books concerning Christian attitudes toward marriage, this one includes a comprehensive, medically accurate chapter on physical adjustment. Although sex should never be the dominant drive, conflict and confusion in this area frequently result in marital chaos.

Most significantly, Pastor LaHaye stresses the central role of Christ in the home. With the submission of a man and a woman to God's will, marriage is a beautiful, exciting adventure. Without God as the unifying ingredient, it is incomplete.

Even for the reader who has not had the privilege of hearing Pastor LaHaye teach biblical truths Sunday after Sunday, the book will be stimulating and provocative. After studying these chapters, you will be acquainted with God's concern for man and his home. I trust it will be as helpful for you as it has for so many in San Diego, California.

Frank E. Young, M.D., PH.D.

INTRODUCTION

Marriage can be the most happy, mediocre, or unhappy of life's experiences. God designed the opposite sexes to complement each other. He wanted a man and woman to be joined in marriage so that they might each give to the other what each one lacked. But these differences that can complement and blend two unique individuals into one can also be incompatibilities that divide and cause separation instead of oneness. Sex and marriage are often referred to as "doing what comes naturally," but evidence that it is not an instinctive relationship is found in the great unhappiness of many married people. The high divorce rate in the United States is one indication of much marital unhappiness.

The daily parts and pieces of marriage do not automatically fall into place as the romantic glamor of Hollywood indicates. Loving and living with your partner takes daily determination and practice—and the giving of oneself for the good of the other.

Since God created man and woman for each other it follows that the best advice on marriage is in the Bible. God planned marriage for man's good: "And the Lord God said, It is not good that the man should be alone; I will make him an help meet for him....And Adam said, This is now bone of my bones, and flesh of my flesh: she shall be called Woman, because she was taken out of Man. Therefore shall a man leave his father and his mother, and shall cleave unto his wife: and they shall be one flesh" (Genesis 2:18, 23-24).

Man was the only creature God created alone in the Garden; all the animals were made male and female and had mates. However, human beings were created in the image of

God (Genesis 1:26) and given an eternal soul (Genesis 2:7) and a mere mate was not sufficient for man's emotional and spiritual needs. Thus, God planned for a man and woman to be more than mates—to be *helpmates*. Herein lies the secret of a happy marriage. If all two people have in common is the "mating urge" theirs will always be an inadequate relationship scarcely more satisfying than the relationship of animals. In order for man to find ultimate happiness in marriage he and his wife must work together to make their mental, spiritual, emotional, and physical differences blend into a harmonious relationship.

A couple starts out their marriage very much in love. Because of their natural differences, which gradually become more and more apparent, conflict comes into their relationship. If they don't learn how to resolve these conflicts their love will be replaced by hostility and animosity, reducing their chance for a happy marriage.

The late Dr. M. R. DeHaan, Bible teacher and medical doctor, stated, "The nearest thing to heaven on this earth is the Christian family and the home where husband and wife, and parents and children, live in love and peace together for the Lord and for each other. The nearest thing to hell on earth is an ungodly home, broken by sin and iniquity, where parents bicker, quarrel and separate, and children are abandoned to the devil and all the forces of wickedness."[1]

One of the most common causes of emotionally disturbed people today is the average American home. Instead of experiencing security-building love between their parents, children all too often see and feel the traumas of hostility, hatred, and animosity between the two people they love most: their mother and father. From this hostility children

[1]"The Christian Home," by M. R. DeHaan (Grand Rapids, Radio Bible Class), p. 3.

develop emotional insecurity and fears that follow them all through life.

God's plan for home life is different from this general experience. He wants the home to be a haven of love where husband and wife and children live with a sense of security and a feeling of acceptance. With all the turmoil and violence outside the home, everyone needs some place in life where he is surrounded by peace and love. God ordained the home as that place of emotional safety. Everyone who marries wants that kind of home, but a happy home doesn't just happen. It is the result of two things: proper adjustment to each other and incorporation into daily life of the principles of marriage outlined by God in the Bible.

The principles in the following pages are the culmination of research and counseling with hundreds of couples before and after marriage. I have seen "miracles" in the lives of the couples who were willing to follow them. These couples have achieved a happy marriage.

Many couples after receiving premarital or problem-marital counseling have said, "I wish these instructions were in print so we could go home and study them together." Their wishes are now fulfilled in this book. My prayer is that God will use it to help many couples adjust to each other and fill their home with love, warmth and understanding and that they will be "happy though married."

He is everything she wishes to be, and she is just what he would secretly like to be...

1/OPPOSITES ATTRACT

"What makes people like us marry in the first place?" asked a Christian woman after thirteen years of marriage. "We have a hopeless personality conflict! Both of us can be relaxed and gracious when around others, but when together we seem to bring out the worst in each other." Although this example is more extreme than most of the Christian couples I have counseled, it has been apparent to me for years that opposite personalities attract each other.

To understand why this attraction is true, we should be acquainted with what makes people different. Many suggestions have been offered: background, training, nationality, education, etc. These things have a bearing on our differences, but so does our inherited temperament. In my book SPIRIT-CONTROLLED TEMPERAMENT[1] I discussed the four basic temperaments of people and detailed their strengths and weaknesses. My purpose was to show that the Holy Spirit working in the life of a Christian is able to help him overcome his weaknesses. Here I will present a condensed description of the four temperaments to show why opposites attract each other.

Human temperament is a fascinating study! Temperament includes the combination of inborn traits that subcon-

---

[1]Tim F. LaHaye, SPIRIT-CONTROLLED TEMPERAMENT (Wheaton, Illinois, Tyndale House Publishers, 1967)

sciously affect a person's behavior. These traits, passed on by the genes, include intelligence, race, sex, and many other factors. The alignment of temperament traits stems from four basic types. Most of us are a mixture of temperaments, representing characteristics of both parents and grandparents. Usually one temperament type predominates in an individual, but strains of one or two of the others will always be found. Extroverts are predominantely sanguine or choleric in temperament, while introverts are predominantely melancholy or phlegmatic.

THE SANGUINE TEMPERAMENT

A person with the *sanguine* temperament is warm, buoyant, and lively. He is naturally receptive, and external impressions easily find their way to his heart. His emotions rather than reflective thoughts are the basis of most of his decisions.

He enjoys people, does not like solitude, and is at his best when surrounded by friends, where he is "the life of the party." He has an endless repertoire of interesting stories which he tells dramatically, making him a favorite with children as well as adults, and usually making him most welcome at parties or social gatherings.

Mr. Sanguine is never at a loss for words. He often speaks before thinking, but his open sincerity has a disarming effect on many of his listeners, causing them to respond to his mood. His free-wheeling, seemingly exciting, extroverted way of life often makes him the envy of the more timid temperament types.

His noisy, blustering, friendly ways make him appear more confident than he really is, but his energy and lovable disposition get him by the rough spots of life. People have a way of excusing his weaknesses by saying, "That's just the way he is."

The world is enriched by these cheerful, enjoyable sanguine people. They make good salesmen, hospital workers, teachers, conversationalists, actors, public speakers, and leaders.

Mr. Sanguine is usually voted 'The Man Most Likely to Succeed," but he often falls short of this prediction. His weakness of will may make him ineffective and undependable. He tends to be restless, undisciplined, egotistical, and emotionally explosive.

THE CHOLERIC TEMPERAMENT

The *choleric* temperament is found in the hot, quick, active, practical, and strong-willed person. He tends to be self-sufficient, independent, decisive, and opinionated, finding it easy to make decisions for himself as well as for other people.

Mr. Choleric thrives on activity. In fact, to him, "life is activity." He does not need to be stimulated, but rather stimulates his environment with his endless ideas, plans, and ambitions. His continual activity is not aimless because he has a practical, keen mind that is capable of making instant decisions and planning worthwhile long-range projects. He does not vacillate under the pressure of what others think. He takes a definite stand on issues and can often be found crusading for some great social cause.

He is seldom frightened by adversities; in fact, they tend to encourage him. He possesses dogged determination and often succeeds where others fail, not because his plans are better than theirs, but because he is still pushing ahead after others have become discouraged and quit. If there is any truth in the adage, "Leaders are born, not made," then he is a born leader.

Mr. Choleric's emotional nature is the least developed part of his temperament. He does not sympathize easily with others, nor does he naturally show or express compassion. Indeed, he is often embarrassed or disgusted by the tears of others. He has little appreciation for the fine arts because his primary interest lies in the utilitarian values of life.

He is quick to recognize opportunities and equally as quick at diagnosing the best way to make use of them. Even though he has a well-organized mind, details usually bore him. He is not given to analysis, but rather to quick, almost intuitive appraisal; therefore, he tends to look at the goal for which he is working without seeing the potential pitfalls and obstacles in the path. Once he has started toward his goal, he will run roughshod over individuals who stand in his way. He tends to be domineering and is often considered an opportunist.

Many of the world's great generals and leaders have been cholerics. They make good executives, idea men, producers, dictators, or criminals, depending upon their moral standards. Like Mr. Sanguine, the choleric individual is an extrovert, although somewhat less intense.

His weaknesses usually make him a difficult person to live with, for he may be hot-tempered, cruel, impetuous, and self-sufficient. The person with this temperament is often more appreciated by friends and associates than by members of his family.

THE MELANCHOLY TEMPERAMENT

The "black, or dark temperament" often characterizes

the melancholy person. The melancholy person is an analytical, self-sacrificing, gifted perfectionist with a very sensitive emotional nature. No one gets more enjoyment from the fine arts than the melancholy.

By nature he is prone to be an introvert, but has a variety of moods because he is usually dominated by his emotions. Sometimes his moods will lift him to heights of ecstasy and cause him to act in a more extroverted manner. However, at other times he will become gloomy and depressed, and during these periods he is withdrawn and can be quite antagonistic.

Mr. Melancholy is a faithful friend, but unlike Mr. Sanguine he does not make friends easily. He will not push himself forward to meet people, but rather waits for people to come to him. He is perhaps the most dependable of all the temperaments, for his perfectionist tendencies do not permit him to be a shirker or let others down when they are depending on him. His natural reluctance to put himself forward is not an indication that he doesn't like people, for like the rest of us, he not only likes others but has a strong desire to be loved by them. But disappointing experiences make him reluctant to take people at their face value; and thus, he is suspicious when others seek him out or shower him with attention.

His exceptional analytical ability causes him to diagnose accurately the obstacles and dangers of any project he has a part in planning. This foresight contrasts sharply with the choleric person who rarely anticipates problems or difficulties but is confident he is able to cope with whatever problems that may arise. This characteristic often finds the melancholy either hesitant to initiate some new project or in conflict with those who wish to. Occasionally, when he is in one of his moods of emotional ecstasy or inspiration, he may produce some great work of art or genius. These accomplishments are often followed by periods of great depression.

Mr. Melancholy usually finds his greatest meaning in life through personal sacrifice. He seems to have a desire to make himself suffer and will often choose a difficult vocation involving great personal sacrifice. Once the decision is made, he is prone to be very thorough and persistent in his pursuit of it and is more than likely to accomplish great good.

The melancholy person has much natural potential when energized by the Holy Spirit. Many of the world's great artists, musicians, inventors, philosophers, educators, and theoreticians are of the melancholy temperament.

The weaknesses of the melancholy individual are numerous: he tends to be self-centered, sensitive, pessimistic, critical, moody, and vengeful. This temperament has induced most of the world's geniuses and some of the most worthless of men, depending on whether the person emphasized his strengths or was overwhelmed by his weaknesses. They often have more problems making emotional adjustments to life than others, and when overwhelmed by their weaknesses are consumed by persecution complexes, excessive guilt complexes, depression, hypochondria, groundless fears, and hostility.

THE PHLEGMATIC TEMPERAMENT

The phlegmatic temperament is calm, cool, slow, easygoing, and well-balanced. Life for the phlegmatic person is a happy, unexciting, pleasant experience in which he avoids involvement with others as much as possible.

Mr. Phlegmatic seldom seems to get ruffled—and rarely expresses anger or laughter. He is the one temperament type that is steadily consistent. Beneath a cool, reticent, almost timid personality, Mr. Phlegmatic has a good combination of abilities. He feels much more emotion than appears on the surface and has a good capacity to appreciate the fine arts and the better things of life.

Because he enjoys people, Mr. Phlegmatic does not lack for friends. He has a dry sense of humor that can have a crowd in stitches while he never cracks a smile. He has the unique capability of seeing something humorous in others and the things they do. His retentive mind makes him a good imitator—and he delights in needling or poking fun at the other temperament types. Annoyed by the aimless, restless enthusiasm of the sanguine, he often confronts him with the futility of such enthusiasm. He is disgusted by the gloomy moods of the melancholy and is prone to ridicule him. He enjoys throwing ice water on the bubbling plans and ambitions of the choleric.

He tends to be a spectator in life and tries not to get too involved with the activities of others. In fact, it is usually with great reluctance that he is motivated to any form of activity beyond his daily routine. This does not mean, however, that he cannot appreciate the need for action or the difficulties of others. He and Mr. Choleric may see the same social injustice, but their responses will be entirely different. The crusading spirit of the choleric will cause him to say, "Let's get a committee organized and campaign to do something about this!" Mr. Phlegmatic would be more likely to respond by saying, "These conditions are terrible! Why doesn't someone do something about them?"

Mr. Phlegmatic is usually kindhearted and sympathetic, but seldom conveys his true feelings. He will not take leadership on his own, but when it is put upon him he proves an excellent leader because he has a conciliating effect on others and is a natural peacemaker.

17

The world has greatly benefited by the gracious nature of the efficient phlegmatic. He makes a good diplomat, accountant, teacher, leader, scientist, or other meticulous type of worker.

The phlegmatic's chief weakness, and the one that often keeps him from fulfilling his potential, is lack of motivation —or laziness. Content with watching others play the games of life, he teases them as a means of protecting himself or conserving his energies. In addition, he is stubborn, indecisive, and fearful.

He is usually easy to live with, but his careless, low-pressure way of life can be a source of irritation to an aggressive partner. Phlegmatics usually make good companions to their children; it is easier for them to stop what they are doing and play with the children than for the activist temperaments. Many a hard-driving husband will say of his phlegmatic wife, "She is a wonderful wife and mother but a lousy housekeeper." Conversely, the flawless housewife may be a poor mother. She would like to stop and play with the children, but the floor needs scrubbing, the clothes need washing, the....These subconscious reactions to life-situations are a part of our temperaments.

Temperament is important to this study on marital happiness because it helps explain why people are so different. It also offers a key as to why opposites attract each other.

WHY OPPOSITES ATTRACT

The subconscious mind has far more influence on us than most people realize. This is graphically seen in the way we usually select our friends—and particularly by our choice of a life partner. The loud, gregarious, extroverted sanguine subconsciously wishes he could control himself better. When he returns from a party, he is often secretly embarrassed by his endless chatter and domination of conversations. The sweet, quiet phlegmatic or melancholic person subconsciously thinks, "I wish I could be more outgoing and expressive." It is very easy to see why these contrasting types will be interested in each other when they meet. He is everything she wishes to be, and she is just what he would secretly like to be; thus, they seem to naturally complement each other. This principle is subconsciously at work almost every time a person singles out the one he wants to marry. In fact, no temperament is subconsciously barred to a person but his own. The important thing to note is that people are attracted to each other on the basis of strengths, but each natural strength has a corresponding weakness.

WEAKNESSES APPEAR LATER

Most couples are so much in love they see only the strengths of the other person before marriage. After the novelty of marriage is over, however, each partner's weaknesses (and every human being has them) begin to appear. These weaknesses call for adjustment—that is, learning to live with the partner's weaknesses. It is important for a married couple to have the Holy Spirit's help so that they might be "gentle, patient, kind, and self-controlled" while adjusting to these weaknesses. Also, the Holy Spirit helps turn weaknesses into positive attributes. Galatians 5:22-23 points out nine characteristics available to the Spirit-filled[2] Christian: a strength for every natural weakness. A Spirit-filled Christian attains more enjoyment in his marriage because he uses the Holy Spirit's help to overcome his weak-

[2]See Appendix A for the author's explanation of what it means to be Spirit-filled.

nesses; and thus, he becomes less objectionable to his partner. In addition, the Holy Spirit gives him grace to overlook and joyously live with his partner's weaknesses.

Personality Conflicts

Personality conflicts are in reality conflicting weaknesses and could be called *temperament conflicts.* They are weaknesses in one partner that irritate the weaknesses in the other. Here are some examples I have encountered in counseling.

Mr. Sanguine's carelessness and unfinished projects create a great conflict for his wife's melanchony, perfectionist, and faithful tendencies. When he comes home late from a sales meeting and his wife has had supper waiting for two hours, she has a hard time "forgiving and forgetting" his thoughtlessness. After a few years she gets tired of his exaggerated stories and careless handling of the truth. Her narration is not nearly as interesting as his—"But at least it is true!"

Mr. Choleric gives his active mind to the business of making a living, and his wife feels neglected. She doesn't realize that before marriage she was his project and that he had given himself 100 percent, as he usually does, to reaching his goal of marrying her. Now that the "marriage project" is accomplished, he is off on the next step in his plan, to support her. If she is careless, he may get very irritated at her disorganization and lash her with cruel, sarcastic words. He now sees her gracious, calm manner—as he thought of her before marriage—as "laziness and lack of motivation."

Mrs. Melancholy often falls into a black mood shortly after marriage. The natural letdown after the tense, exciting anticipation of her wedding can lead to a period of depression. If her husband is impatient and frustrated, she may lapse into silence, hypochondria, or weeping. Her supersensitivity can make her suspicious that "he doesn't love me any more." Her perfectionism when motivated into house-keeping can create a flawlessly kept house in which her husband can seldom feel relaxed and at home. She can get upset if he puts his feet on the coffee table or doesn't pick up his socks. One of her biggest temptations is to keep all of her frustrations bottled up inside her, where they ultimately "explode" or produce nervousness, ulcers or other maladies.

Mr. Phlegmatic's lack of motivation becomes a drain on his partner. A natural "stay at home" type, he can become boring unless he learns to push himself for his partner's sake. However, he can begin an activity "just for the wife's sake" and, before he realizes it, have a good time himself. He does a good job of house repairs—if she can ever get him going. One choleric mother I know gave her choleric daughter, married to a phlegmatic husband, this sage advice: "Shirley, when you get him up, keep him moving." A phlegmatic partner is less inclined to be generous than a sanguine, and this factor added to quiet stubbornness can create great resentment and frustration.

Manage Your Conflicts

Differences between partners need not be fatal! No disagreement is a threat to a marriage; it's what a couple does about disagreements that determines the success or failure of a marriage. Many a good marriage today once experienced vigorous temperament conflicts.

The following suggestions are given to help you make the right kind of adjustments.

• When you feel frustration, resentment, or some other form of hostility, stop and take an objective look at what causes it.

• Pray about it. First, confess your sin of grieving the Holy Spirit (Ephesians 4:30-32). Your peace of mind does not depend on your partner's behavior. After facing your inner hostility and anger as sin and confessing it (I John 1:9), ask God to fill you with his Spirit (Luke 11:13) then walk in the Spirit (Galatians 5:16). Second, pray about your partner's actions, asking God to help him see his shortcomings and to lead you in discussing the matter with him.

• Communicate with your partner about his fault. This should always be done "in love" (Ephesians 4:15). Pick a relaxed time when you can objectively share your feelings without getting overly emotional. Never speak in anger, and always allow time for him to think about what you've said. Then leave the matter up to the Holy Spirit.

• Ask God, the giver of love, to fill you with love for him and for your partner so that you can genuinely love him in spite of his weaknesses. Look at his strengths and thank God for them (I Thessalonians 5:18).

• Forget past mistakes and sins! "Forgetting those things which are behind, and reaching forth unto those things which are before, I press toward the mark for the prize of the high calling of God in Christ Jesus" (Philippians 3:13b-14).

If you repeatedly follow this procedure, you will find that your reaction to your partner's actions will be led by the Holy Spirit and your love will increase so that, like paint, it will cover a multitude of weaknesses.

Do you want your wife to treat you like a king? Then treat her like a queen!

2 FORGET YOURSELF

"We don't intend to have children for at least two years! That way we will have time to adjust to each other before we must learn to adjust to children." This statement is one of the most common answers I get to my usual question in pre-marital counseling, "What are your thoughts about raising a family?" It points out the generally recognized fact that most couples expect to go through a period of adjustment in their marriage. This period usually lasts about three years. Some years ago a survey on divorce revealed that seven out of ten divorces occurred within the first three years of marriage. Most happily married couples will agree that although their first three years contained many blessed and happy times they also contained many difficult adjustment experiences.

Most marriage counselors acknowledge three basic areas of marital adjustment—mental, physical, and spiritual. Proper adjustment in each of these areas is necessary to create a well-rounded marriage. If we were to let a circle represent the total marriage, then each of the three adjustment areas would represent about one-third of the total relationship. Although the age of the couple when married and the length of the marriage are factors which can make one area more important than another, over a lifetime of marriage the three areas are approximately equal in importance. In the twenties the physical may dominate the others, but in the thirties the mental often dominates the physical and spiritual, and from the late thirties on the spiritual usually dominates the others.

These three adjustment areas are always interdependent. It is unusual for couples to have good physical adjustment if they do not have a high degree of mental adjustment. I have known couples whose difficulty in adjusting mentally produced physical maladjustment, but because of their strong spiritual relationship—through faith in Christ—they were able to make better mental and physical adjustments. The spiritual is potentially the most important because it can radically improve the adjustment in the other two.

Because of the great significance of these three adjustment areas, I will deal with them individually in successive chapters, beginning with the mental adjustment area.

The mental adjustment in marriage, while usually the most complex, offers an exciting opportunity for two people to get to know each other deeply. Due to the fact that individuals are prone to be on their best behavior all through courtship, most married couples have tremendous mental adjustments to make. This area of adjustment highlights background differences and encompasses a variety of experiences that require retraining.

In physically adjusting a couple starts out learning a whole new experience. In the spiritual realm they can, through the study of the Word of God, similarly learn a new relationship to each other and to God. But in the mental area each has spent approximately twenty or more years adjusting to other people according to his own pattern. Now they come into marriage, with its responsibilities and natural pressures, and may find that their adjustment patterns to certain experiences are in conflict with their partner's. Therefore, take special note of the golden rule of mental adjustment as found in Philippians 2:3-4:

> Let nothing be done through strife or vainglory; but in lowliness of mind let each esteem other better than themselves. Look not every man on his own things, but every man also on the things of others.

With determination before God to forget yourself and make your partner happy as these verses teach, you cannot help but make wholesome adjustments to the many mental facets of married life. I shall discuss five of the most common problems of mental adjustment.

FINANCES

Financial adjustment is perhaps the most difficult, partially because most couples have been so dependent upon their parents. The situation is further confused today by both husband and wife working. If the wife has worked prior to marriage and kept her own checking account, it is natural that she may want to do the same afterward. If she is going to work to help her husband finish his education, she may assume the role of breadwinner and look down on her husband rather than recognize that her endeavor is an investment in their lifetime vocation—an investment that will pay lifelong dividends.

Who Should Handle The Money?

The answer to this question is far more significant than just dollars and cents. God has stated very clearly in his

Word that the man should be the head of the house. This principle produces happiness; violation of the principle produces misery. I have never known a happy henpecked husband, nor have I ever met a happy henpecker. God would never ask a woman to be in subjection to her husband unless it was for her good. A woman will not be lastingly happy unless she is in subjection to her husband.

Why is this important in relationship to finances? Simply because of the truth of an age-old adage, "He that holds the purse strings rules the family." You will find that the treasurer of any organization often has an inordinate consciousness of power. This is particularly true in a family. Whether the wife is a trained bookkeeper and the husband a terrible mathematician has nothing to do with it. The husband should handle the finances in a marriage, particularly for the first seven to ten years.

This does not mean that the wife should not have her area of responsibility. A couple can plan a budget that provides the wife with a set amount for food, household expenses, her miscellaneous needs and such other things as they agree upon. The husband then should pay the bills, balance the bank account and be responsible for the overall financial structure. They should not have separate bank accounts; if the wife works she should put her earnings into the family account. Large purchases of furniture, appliances, cars, etc., should be by joint agreement. Anytime one of the partners is opposed to a particular financial investment, it would be far better to wait until there is agreement than to have one defy the other's feelings on the matter.

The Working Wife

It is increasingly popular for wives to work. Many young

couples think that getting started in marriage, saving enough to make a down payment on a home, or helping a husband through college are acceptable reasons for a wife to work. This arrangement should only be until children come into the home. However, when a wife works, certain dangers arise that should be considered.

The most important is that if the wife works and keeps her money separate from her husband's, it breeds a feeling of independence and self-sufficiency which God did not intend a married woman to have. This feeling makes it difficult for her to adjust to her husband during the early stages of marriage. I am convinced that one of the reasons young married couples divorce so readily today is because the wife is not economically dependent upon her husband; whenever difficulties and pressures arise she can say, as one young lady said to me, "I don't have to take that kind of thing; I can live by myself!" I always recommend that a joint bank account be kept and that a working wife keep from her paycheck only what she needs for her living and household expenses. Marriage is a joint venture between two people who live as one. It is not two distinct corporations doing business under the same roof.

The second danger to a working wife is that the birth of children is often delayed too long. If you wait until you can afford to have children, you will probably never have them. They are such a source of enrichment and blessing in a family that young people should plan early on having them and work toward that date; otherwise you may cheat yourselves out of the blessing of parenthood and thus be disobedient to God's command that we "...be fruitful, and multiple, and replenish the earth..." (Genesis 1:28).

Indebtedness

One of the severe problems in many marriages is that within a few weeks after marriage a couple find themselves hopelessly in debt. This financial strain produces tensions and fears that are an unnecessary hindrance to a proper adjustment. Avoid impulse buying; obligate yourselves only for the absolute essentials. Someone has suggested that monthly payments should never exceed ten percent of a couple's income, in addition to automobile and house payments. The wife's attitude toward possessions is very important in the early stages of marriage; she can unconsciously drive her husband to overextend himself in an effort to please her. She should avoid comparisons between the home her father was able to provide and the little apartment and frugal conditions under which she starts marriage. Remember that parents have had twenty years or more in which to accumulate the possessions they enjoy, and in due time you may hope for the same. The wife's patience and joyous acceptance of her husband's financial capabilities are among the ways she can invest in a long-lasting and happy marriage.

Fiscal Responsibility

A responsible fiscal program for the Christian couple was beautifully described by Charlie W. Shedd in "Letters to Karen," (his daughter) published in Reader's Digest, January, 1966, in which he gave this motto: "Give ten percent, save ten percent, and spend the rest with thanksgiving and praise!"

As a Christian couple, start out immediately securing God's blessing on your family finances according to Malachi 3:3-11 by giving him one-tenth of your income. You can literally accomplish more financially with God's blessing on the expenditure of 90 percent than you can the 100 percent without God's blessing. I have never known a couple that was not blessed by tithing. "...prove me now herewith, saith the Lord of hosts, if I will not open you the windows of heaven, and pour you out a blessing, that there shall not be room enough to receive it" (Malachi 3:10).

By saving the second ten percent, you will find it possible to pay cash for some of the items you need without expensive interest charges and the pressure of payments. If you do not start out your marriage with these two practices, you may find it difficult to start later. However, it is not impossible. Give God the tithe and trust him to guide you through your financial problems. He never fails.

SOCIAL LIFE

Another significant area of mental adjustment is your social life. God created human beings for fellowship with himself and with one another. However, you will find that differences in social likes and dislikes—that you never dreamed existed—will appear after marriage. One sports-enthusiast husband and his music-loving wife had this conversation about a year after they were married. He asked, "Why is it that you don't go to football games with me any more?" She replied, "Well, I really don't understand football and I just don't enjoy it." With exasperation he retorted, "I don't understand that. When we were going together you never turned me down when I invited you to go to a game and you always seemed to enjoy it." Her reply was enlightening. "Oh, that's easy to understand. I enjoyed being with you so much I didn't care where we went." She then asked, "Why it is that you don't take me to concerts any more the way you did when we were going together?" He replied, "I can't stand longhair music!"

Suddenly they both realized that in their courtship days their love for each other had anesthetized them to their social differences. The thrill and excitement of being together made unpleasant things enjoyable. This kind of enlightenment will appear to almost every couple in several areas of their social life after marriage. By facing their differences and "in honor preferring one another," this couple worked out a policy wherein the wife went with the husband to sporting events and the husband took the wife to some musicals. By patiently learning the significance of the third-down play, she began not only to understand football, but to become an avid fan. He in turn has gained a greater appreciation for classical music so that a concert is no longer "sheer torture" to him.

We are all subject to change, and many times our likes and dislikes are based purely on prejudice or bad experiences in the past. Being creatures of habit, we can cultivate new likes and dislikes by enthusiastically throwing ourselves into something for "love's sake."

Friends Are Important

Couples eventually seek the companionship of other couples. They soon find that his boyfriends and her girl friends have differing interests and time schedules so that gradually, unless the friends also marry, they make a new set of friends and associates.

Friends have a great influence upon us, particularly as we socialize with them. It is most important, therefore, that Christians find some Christian friends as close companions. You will have other friends, too. Ask the Holy Spirit to help you introduce them to Christ. But you will need Christian friends to help you grow in faith.

The best place to find Christian companionship is in

your church. Take an active part in the Sunday school and become involved in the couples' group of your age. Use your home to entertain other couples and be a friend to them. The old principle, "He that would have friends must show himself friendly," is also true for couples. One thing to bear in mind is that social life should not stop after marriage. Naturally, you will not have the whirlwind social life you experienced as a single person in your courting days, because now your money is being spent for more permanent things. Nevertheless, you need to relax together outside of the home occasionally. This area is another one in which adjustment can be made by communication and loving consideration.

FAMILY

Your relationship to your partner's family is important. Occasionally a partner's parents will be so ideal that he never has problems with them, but frankly, that is an exception rather than the rule. Most parents find it difficult to clip all apron strings after their children marry, even though they know they should. A couple should live separately from their parents, but be very respectful toward them. It is most natural for parents to offer advice based on their twenty or more years of experience, and sometimes couples rebel at this even to the point of rejecting good advice because it came from one of their parents.

Usually one's own parents are not as annoying as the partner's parents, simply because each one understands his own parents better. Many times an in-law's suggestions appear to be disapproval or judgment when in reality they were given with the best of intentions.

33

You can afford to be considerate and thoughtful of your partner's parents. After all, they spent many years and thousands of dollars preparing your mate. The least you can do is treat them with dignity and respect. Avoid speaking negatively to your partner's parents; if it is necessary to tell them they are interfering too much in your marriage, always let their offspring do the telling. It is probably wise that husband and wife go together, but the blood relative should state the situation.

The maternal instinct being what it is, mothers frequently have greater difficulty giving up their sons than do fathers their daughters. A loving wife should try to understand this and not put her husband into the difficult position of having to choose the one to whom he will be loyal, his wife or his mother. By thoughtfulness and love the wife can help the husband maintain a relaxed feeling toward his parents and particularly his mother. This considerateness will also benefit the wife. She can afford to be generous in this area. She has her husband now for much more time than his mother had him, and besides, she has a relationship to him that can never be shared by another woman, including his mother.

A husband should be very careful to avoid comparisons between his wife and his mother. It is entirely unfair to compare a young wife's ironing, cooking, and housekeeping abilities to those of a woman who has had twenty years of experience. Indulgence in unkind comparisons of this nature will only create hostilities and conflict between the two women most important to the husband.

Difficulties in family relationships should be talked over carefully and dealt with lovingly. It is possible, with God's help, to have an enjoyable relationship with in-laws that in turn enriches your marriage.

APPEARANCE

Many a joke has been made about brides who come to to the table with "stringy hair, sleepy eyes and unpainted face" on the first morning after marriage. This moment of truth is no joking matter! Appearance isn't everything, but nevertheless it is important. The Bible tells us that "man looketh on the outward appearance, but the Lord looketh on the heart" (I Samuel 16:7). Since your partner is human, he or she is going to look on your "outward appearance." It is therefore important that you do not use a wedding certificate as an excuse to relax your standards of appearance.

You would, no doubt, never have been attractive to your partner if you were not clean and neat in appearance. Help keep your partner's love alive by continuing to look well-groomed whenever possible. Your partner wants to be proud to introduce you to his or her friends; don't make your partner feel like apologizing for your appearance.

Men have a natural tendency to relax on their day off by not shaving. A look in the mirror will reveal that he scarcely looks his best in this unshaven condition. It is usually selfishness that causes a man not to shave on the day that he is with his wife the most—just because it is easier for him.

A bride should begin one ritual immediately after her honeymoon: the last thirty minutes before her husband returns from work she should spend on her appearance. His homecoming should be the high point in her day, and if she plans toward it she will always appear at first sight after his day's work the way she did when they were courting. This personal care is particularly needed in this day of men and women working together. A quick look in any office will reveal that working women try to look their best during the eight hours they are working with other women's husbands. If a wife lets her appearance run down, she puts herself in an unfavorable comparison to these women, and she may be just following the path of least resistance, which is a form of selfishness. Even after you have children, avoid using them as an excuse for shoddy or careless appearance—maintain your attractiveness to your companion.

COURTESY
Courtesy and manners are a grace that should become a part of every Christian's life, but in our modern civilization they seem to be a dying art. Courtesy is something taught a child by his parents and something a girl is able to demand of a boyfriend. The obvious time to discuss your differences on this matter is before marriage. Poor table manners and lack of normal courtesies can be a great source of irritation.

When my mother insisted that we always wear a shirt to the table, refrain from putting our elbows on the table, say please to one another, and use good manners in our treatment of each other, she remarked, "You will never be in better company than the company you are in right now." I am most grateful for her insistence upon these things, because I married a wife who enjoys courtesy and politeness —and I am inclined to believe that most women do.

A woman likes to be treated like a lady; therefore, a husband should be very careful not to stop giving his wife "preferential treatment" after they are married. It is a wise husband who opens doors, including car doors, for his wife and generally treats her as a gentleman should treat a lady. You will be making an investment in her happiness and self-respect, which will increase her love for you. Since love begets love, this is one of the best investments you can make in your marriage.

While holding a family conference in a church in Arizona, I announced one night that the next evening I would tell men "how to get your wife to treat you like a king." For some strange reason we had our largest crowd that night. My advice startled some of the men by its simplicity, for I said: "Treat her like a queen!"

One almost inexcusable practice in marriage is disloyalty. Have you ever been out socially and heard a wife or husband berate and criticize the partner in front of mutual friends? This embarrassing practice is engaged in by partners who do not seem to be able to communicate in private and seek the safety of the group to vent their pent-up wrath. It is one of the most damaging wrongs a person can use against his or her partner.

Never, never air your partner's shortcomings, weaknesses, or deficiencies in front of other people. Never criticize him to your friends or relatives. If you are displeased with your partner's behavior on a matter, there are only two with whom you should share it: God and your partner. "But I have to have someone I can tell my problems to" is the usual defensive retort. As a Christian you have someone to whom you can take your problems: your heavenly Father. Then through prayer and the leading of the Holy Spirit, share the problems with your partner. If this does not work, talk the matter over with your pastor or counselor.

A lovely Christian mother whose daughter married one of the finest young men in our church came to see me one day. She was troubled over her feeling of animosity and bitterness toward her son-in-law and was finding it increasingly difficult to be nice to him. After talking to her and her daughter I found the cause. Two weeks after the couple returned from their honeymoon they had a fight. The daughter called her mother and told her the whole story. That night the husband came home and apologized for his short-tempered treatment of his bride, and they had one of those wonderful "making up" experiences that is such a uniting blessing in marriage.

A few weeks later another argument occurred, and she called her mother during the day to pour out her troubled heart. Without realizing it she called her mother only to tell about the problems they had; she had not called her back to tell about the tender moments of "making up." Consequently, after a few months the mother had only one side of the story of their relationship. It was no wonder that she thought of her new son-in-law as an "ill-tempered brute." By sharing the joys of her marriage with her mother thereafter, the daughter put an end to her mother's resentment toward the son-in-law.

You should never criticize your partner to others for two reasons. First, rehearsing grudges or nursing gripes stamps them more indelibly upon your mind. Second, the desire for approval is one of the basic drives of man. Nothing can make a person feel less approved of than to find that his partner has been so disloyal as to criticize him to an outsider. If needed your pastor or a professional counselor can be consulted, but don't discuss the situation with anyone else.

BE OPEN TO CHANGE

Most spontaneous decisions or prejudices are the result of our background, but that does not determine whether they are right or wrong. I have met men who—because their father did not treat their mother that way—refuse to give in to their wife's desire that they be more gentlemanly and polite. Actually, that reason has nothing to do with it. Just because a man's father made a lifetime of mistakes is no reason his son should perpetuate them. Therefore, whenever you go into a communication session with your partner regarding the mental adjustments of your marriage, always bear in mind that the standards and concepts produced by your background could be wrong. There may be another way of doing it. Remember, one of the characteristics of love is "love seeketh not her own..." (I Corinthians 13:5).

Adjusting in marriage can be a thrilling experience through which you can improve yourself by embracing the strengths of your partner's background and temperament. Be willing to bend and give. Don't resist change in your behavior unless it is behavior for which the Scripture has already set a standard. Be objective about the differences between you and your partner, because just as you expect him to change in some areas, he has a right to expect change from you. Fortunately, change is a natural part of life. One of the happy observations I have made is that many of our "likes" today were "hates" ten years ago. Give your partner time to adjust, and you will find that time draws two unselfish people together.

Unique communication: a person says things and shares burdens in prayer that he would not be able to share on any other level.

3/SPIRITUAL ADJUSTMENT

Man is an intensely spiritual creature. The older he gets, the more conscious he becomes of this fact. Pascal, the physicist and philosopher, said, "There is a God-shaped vacuum in the heart of every man which cannot be satisfied by any created thing, but only by God, the Creator, who is made known through Jesus Christ." When Jesus Christ is invited into a person's life as Lord and Savior, this vacuum is filled. Because of the presence of Jesus Christ a person may have communion with God—a communion which will enrich all areas of his life.

Galatians 5:22 describes the work of God's Spirit in the life of a Christian. As a person submits himself to the Holy Spirit, he begins to develop increasing amounts of love, joy, peace, longsuffering, gentleness, goodness, kindness, meekness, faith, and self-control. Jesus points out the universal principle that a person reaps what he sows; therefore, love (or any other attribute) that is consistently given will be returned to the giver. It follows, then, that a couple who are giving and receiving spiritual attributes will most likely have a delightful and satisfying marriage.

I believe the spiritual area is the most important area

of marital adjustment. A person cannot make a satisfying physical adjustment unless he is first mentally adjusted. Mental adjustments have so many complexities and everyone is so vulnerable to selfishness—which retards that adjustment —that problems in this area are not easy to solve. But, I have observed that a good spiritual life will greatly improve mental adjustments. The Bible is still the greatest handbook on human behavior, and as two people are related to the God of the Bible and to his Word, they will find the principles that will aid them in their mental adjustment. Five areas of spiritual adjustment that can make a marriage thrilling are presented for your consideration and use.

CONSISTENT CHRISTIAN BEHAVIOR

You are the key to the spiritual life of your marriage. Dr. Henry Brandt, a Christian psychologist, points out that adequate parents must first be adequate partners, but before you can be an adequate partner you must be an adequate person. Therefore, consistent Christian behavior in the home is a key to spiritual adjustment. What you are in the home is what you really are. Your partner soon finds out exactly what you are. If you are not consistent in your relationship to God, you will not have the right spiritual point of view to make proper mental or physical adjustments.

Great pressure does not change a person; it only brings out what he is. The pressures of the intimacy of home-living bring to the surface unplanned reactions to life. These reactions will show you what you are. For example, if you have a tendency to "blow your top" or scream or cry when you become tense or upset, the situation at hand is usually not as important as your failure to react in a Christian way. God says to you: "My grace is sufficient for you." Selfish reactions are an indication that you are not using this grace that God offers. For example, suppose your partner says something biting and unkind to you; instead of receiving it graciously you respond with unkind words—you have sinned. Your partner has too, but you are not responsible for his sin; you are responsible to God only for your own sin.

In order to act as you want to act and not just react to a situation do not excuse your behavior, regardless of what prompts it. Go to God and confess your sin, asking him to give you a gracious spirit. Then confess your unkind words or behavior to your partner so that your conscience can be clear. When they lie down at night many people become upset because their unkind words come back to haunt them. Unconfessed weaknesses and failures accumulate until a person feels, not that he has temporarily failed, but that he is a failure. He then loses his sense of worth as a person. The person who will face each failure as a sin and gain God's forgiveness (I John 1:9) will not have to cope with a conscience that haunts and accuses him. In fact, those who face and confess their sin—and ask God for his help—will find that he gives a remedy for it. Consider God's promise in I Corinthians 10:13: "But remember this—the wrong desires that come into your life aren't anything new and different. Many others have faced exactly the same problems before you. And no temptation is irresistible. You can trust God to keep the temptation from becoming so strong that you can't stand up against it, for he has promised this and will do what he says. He will show you how to escape temptation's power so that you can bear up patiently against it" (Living New Testament paraphrase).

If you don't react to your partner with angry and harsh words will he abuse and take advantage of you? Usually not.

The Bible states that "a soft answer turns away wrath" (Proverbs 15:1). It takes two to argue; if you refuse, that ends the argument. Much family heartache could be avoided if even one of the members would respond to God's guidance instead of his own selfish desires. This illustration is only one of the many areas in which consistent actions according to God's principles will open up the way for happy marital adjustments.

Consistency in the home is important. A person does not have to be perfect to maintain the respect of his partner, but acting pietistically at church and the opposite at home will forfeit respect.

Lack of consistency is even more pronounced when children come along. After years of observation, I have concluded that our church's best young people come from either consecrated Christian homes or nonchristian homes. As a rule, mediocre Christian homes do not produce consecrated Christian young people. The reason? Inconsistency. Inconsistency is a form of hypocrisy. The child whose parents make no pretenses at being Christian or religious can understand his parents' behavior because obviously they are not Christians. However, the young person who sees his parents take positions of leadership in the local church and then hears them fuss and feud at home will find it difficult to respect their double standards. For this reason it is imperative for a Christian to seek and follow God's directions for daily living. Thinking, talking, and acting in accordance with one's beliefs brings emotional peace as well as consistent behavior.

Personal Devotional Life

Man's spiritual vacuum is filled by the Holy Spirit when

44

he accepts God's provision for his soul: Jesus Christ. Jesus said, "I am the way, the truth and the life: no man comes unto the Father, but by me" (John 14:6). When a person asks Jesus Christ to direct his life, his spiritual life then begins. He then has access to God's help and direction and this new spiritual element in his life offers so much potential for personal change that the Bible says the person is "born again." A person is born first when he is born physically. And he is born a second time when he accepts spiritual life through Jesus Christ. Taking care of one's spiritual life is just as important as taking care of one's physical life. God wants each person to grow in grace and knowledge of the Lord Jesus, and this growth comes only through the Word of God. Just as a person feeds his body three times a day, twenty-one times a week (often whether he thinks he needs it or not), so must he daily feed his soul. And the food needed is the Word of God. Even five to twenty minutes a day spent reading the Bible and meditating on God's words will help one live a consistent Christian life.

YOUR CHURCH LIFE

Many immediately think of the church when they consider the spiritual area of life. Often people do not realize that spirituality is an intensely individual relationship to God. This relationship is not dependent upon the church, but it is definitely aided by the church. God desires that people come together to share their faith and worship him. The church should help people grow as Christians by giving them opportunities to study the Bible, by encouraging them to read it and pray daily, and by giving them opportunities to serve and help other people.

Finding a church home may be simple for the young

couple that has grown up in the same church. If, however, they have grown up in different churches or after their marriage they move to another location, it is necessary to find a church in which both feel at home and in which they can be enthusiastic participants. Each couple should give careful thought to what they want to give and receive from their church. When a couple attend church haphazardly—without a definite purpose or goal—their church experience is often disappointing.

What To Look For In A Church

Eighty-five percent of the people who have joined our church came the first time because they were invited by someone else. In all probability some friend will recommend a church to you, but frankly, that is not adequate reason for joining it. A lot of unnecessary sentimentality and loyalty enter into the selection of a church. Your church home is so important that it should not be selected because of emotional sentiment, but because of spiritual understanding and reasoning. Before you join the church where your children will be receiving much of their spiritual training, check it for the following basic requirements.

• Does it teach the Bible? Does the minister preach from the Bible? Is the Sunday school material adequately based on the Bible? Do the people meet each week for Bible study and prayer? If necessary, it would be better to change your denomination, provided it did not violate your doctrinal convictions, to attend a Bible-teaching church than to remain with your denomination and neglect a sound biblical ministry.

• Is the church concerned that other people find salvation in Jesus Christ? Often such a church will provide an invitation at the close of the service and will conduct occasional evangelistic campaigns. It will also make an earnest attempt to get the members to participate in calling on visitors and those in the community.

• Is it a missionary-minded church? A church that is not concerned with sending out missionaries soon becomes a mission field. Check to see how long it has been since a missionary was called out of that congregation (provided it is not a very young church).

CHRISTIAN SERVICE AND WITNESS

A growing Christian will want to serve Christ. "What? know ye not that your body is the temple of the Holy Ghost which is in you, which ye have of God, and ye are not your own? For ye are bought with a price: therefore glorify God in your body, and in your spirit, which are God's" (I Corinthians 6:19-20). Many young marrieds get so involved in each other and the acquisition of things for their home that they neglect Christian service. Often the young married couples group is the most unspiritual of the adult groups in a church, even though it may have many young people who grew up in the church, because Christ does not have first place in their lives (Matthew 6:33).

A person's church provides an excellent opportunity to serve Christ. Consider serving as a Sunday school teacher or youth worker or in the visitation program. As with everything else in the Christian life, one benefits by what he does for Christ. I have had many a person tell me, "Pastor, since I have been teaching a Sunday school class I have learned far more about the Bible than I ever learned from your sermons." Christian service provides great motivation for studying the Word of God (2 Timothy 2:15), which in turn builds up one's Christian life.

In addition to serving in the church, Jesus Christ wants to use each life as a witness—the wife in the community among other wives and neighbors, the husband among the men with whom he works and at home to the neighbors. Make it a practice to share your faith with other people. Nothing "turns people on" spiritually quite like sharing their faith with someone else. The Lord Jesus Christ said that Christians are his witnesses to other people (Acts 1:8). Many empty lives need the dynamic witness of a consecrated Christian couple.

A FAMILY ALTAR

The family altar can be the most powerful single influence in the home. The couple who comes together already experienced in prayer knows the value and benefits of a prayer time. However, even if one or both partners are inexperienced at prayer, the ideal place to learn to pray is with each other at home. The family altar is also the best place for children to learn to pray. The Lord may well have had the family unit in mind when he gave this promise: "Again I say unto you, That if two of you shall agree on earth as touching any thing that they shall ask, it shall be done for them of my Father which is in heaven. For where two or three are gathered together in my name, there am I in the midst of them" (Matthew 18:19-20).

A family altar is not an ethereal or mysterious experience, but a very simple and practical matter of reading the Bible and praying with family members. In contrast to the current high divorce rate, the following statistics indicate that a family altar draws the family members together in love and understanding. According to a survey of Christian marriages taken by Dr. Pitirim Sorokin of Harvard University, where "the family practice of Bible study and prayer is daily observed, there is only one divorce in every 1015 marriages." It appears that not only is divorce practically eliminated from families that have a family altar, but that much of the heartache and unhappiness associated with present-day marriage finds no place in their homes.

How To Have A Family Altar

The following suggestions are offered to make your family altar a meaningful experience.

• Set a regular time for family devotions and make no exceptions unless absolutely necessary. Decide upon a time, either morning or evening, and create the habit no matter who is in your home. When possible the family altar should be initiated on the wedding night, but it's never too late to start one.

• Read a passage in the Scriptures and, as you feel led, discuss it. Before children come, a chapter a day would be an ideal goal. After children arrive, it is probably better to read less and make what you read meaningful to them.

• Have prayer by both husband and wife, joined by each of the children as they mature. If yours is a missionary-minded church, your family altar is an excellent place to uphold your missionaries on a regular basis. Family prayer should always carry the spirit of thanksgiving and should feature your intercession on behalf of those who cannot pray for themselves, such as unsaved neighbors, backslidden Christians, and the sick—as well as petitions for yourselves. Pray specifically so that you can expect specific answers.

A family altar provides a unique means of communication. A person says things and shares burdens in prayer that he would not be able to share on any other level. Praying together molds two people by the bonds and cords of love in a very thrilling way. United prayer is a way of multiplying and strengthening love through the passing years. One Christian man gave this testimony: "Today, after twenty-six years of marriage, I am more sensitive to the thrill of her presence than I have ever been. When I come on her unexpectedly in a crowd, it is like a glad little song rising up somewhere inside me. When I catch her eye in public, it is as though she were hanging out a sign with the exact word of inspiration I need right then...I still count it the day's biggest thrill when she comes hurrying from wherever she is to greet me. And as I look down the road ahead, I see an elderly man and woman going into the sunset hand-in-hand. I know in my heart that the end will be better by far than the beginning."[2] This experience came because early in their marriage this couple through the family altar had learned to avail themselves of "the secret chamber of divine communion where two lives are blended into a sacred unity."

FORGIVENESS

You have not married a perfect person; neither has your partner! Therefore, you will both have to forgive one another for your mistakes, sins, selfishness, and other forms of thoughtless behavior. Never carry a grudge; it is a burden too heavy to bear. Let your watchword be Ephesians 4:31-32: "Let all bitterness, and wrath, and anger, and clamor, and evil speaking, be put away from you, with all malice: And be ye kind one to another, tenderhearted, forgiving one another,

---

[2]Charlie W. Shedd, LETTERS TO KAREN, (Nashville, Tennessee, Abingdon Press). Used by permission.

even as God for Christ's sake hath forgiven you." An exacting person will find it more difficult to be forgiving than will an easy-going person. However, God expects you to be forgiving. The Lord Jesus made it clear in Matthew 6:14-15 that you cannot be forgiven of your sins unless you are willing to forgive others for theirs. Therefore, forgiveness is a spiritual necessity. You can be sure that your heavenly Father will enable you to do what he has thus commanded you to do—forgive one another regardless of the fault.

Never go to bed angry! The Bible tells us, ". . . let not the sun go down upon your wrath: Neither give place to the devil" (Ephesians 4:26-27). Your willingness to forgive your partner affects both your personal and family life spiritually. Make it your responsibility to initiate forgiveness. It will help you to achieve a strong spiritual home, which in turn will enrich every other area of your marriage.

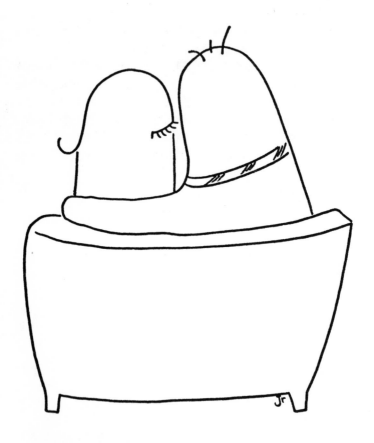

Designed by God for man's good, the act of marriage can be a husband and wife's most sublime expression of love.

4/PHYSICAL JOYS

Physical adjustment in marriage[1] can be properly compared to the instrumental adjustment necessary for an orchestra to produce a beautiful, harmonious symphony. Contrary to popular opinion, "doing what comes naturally" does not automatically guarantee physical harmony in the marriage relationship. Human beings are so much more complex in their emotional structure than animals that their sex drive cannot be compared simply to the mating urge. If "the marriage act," which is the name I prefer rather than the popular title "sex act," is not built upon mutual love and the climax of tender expressions of thoughtfulness and endearment, it will not produce the symphony of emotional harmony that God intended for married couples. Physical discord will lead to frustration for one or both partners.

Lack of mutual harmony in the marriage relationship does not mean that a marriage is doomed to failure. It can mean, however, that something is seriously wrong and that the couple should seek counsel from their pastor, a Christian doctor, or a counselor. Most discord in the marriage act can be attributed to one of three things: ignorance, selfishness, or fear.

Most people have been properly taught modesty from

[1]The author is indebted to several medical friends with whom he discussed this chapter, particularly Dr. William Halcomb, a physician in San Clemente, California, who spent many hours with him and Dr. Frank Young who critically reviewed the manuscript, offered several suggestions, and graciously agreed to write the foreword.

childhood. However, many times this standard of modesty has shrouded in mystery the splendors of the human anatomy. In an effort to dispel that mystery I will seek to be very frank in my presentation of the sexual relationship that exists between a husband and wife. As Dr. Henry Brandt has stated, "God has not made the human body with good parts and bad parts; he has made it all good." That includes the reproductive system, the part of the human anatomy that for many people has not been explained. I would urge you, therefore, to examine the following medical drawings and familiarize yourself with the names and functions of the various reproductive organs for both the male and female. A proper understanding of these bodily functions will greatly aid your physical adjustment. Each organ is listed in the sequence of its reproductive function.

SCROTUM or SCROTAL SAC—the small pouch which hangs between a man's legs containing the testicles.

TESTICLES—the sensitive, egg-shaped sperm-manufacturing organs that hang in the scrotal sac. They contain a long tube, approximately one one-thousandth of an inch in diameter and about one thousand feet long, and are able to produce five hundred thousand sperm every week.

SPERM or SPERMATOZOA—the male seed manufactured in the testicles; the sperm fertilizes the female egg. This seed contains the genetic information which determines the sex of the child. In the marriage act it is ejected through the penis into the female vagina.

EPIDIDYMIS—the little channel in the scrotal sac where sperm manufactured in the testicles undergo a maturing process.

SPERMATIC DUCT (vas deferens)—the duct from the epididy-

THE MALE REPRODUCTIVE ORGANS [2]

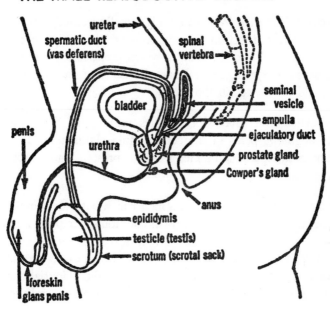

mis which carries the sperm into the ampulla chamber.

AMPULLA CHAMBER—the storage chamber for sperm that has left the epididymis and traveled through the spermatic duct.

SEMINAL VESICLE—the organ which produces the seminal fluid that carries the sperm to the prostate gland.

EJACULATORY DUCT—the organ that explodes the sperm and seminal fluid through the penis into the female.

PROSTATE GLAND—this gland produces additional seminal fluid

[2]Joseph B. Henry, FULFILLMENT IN MARRIAGE (Westwood, New Jersey, Fleming H. Revell Company, 1966), p. 144. Used by permission.

and contains the nerves which control the erection of the penis.

COWPER'S GLAND—When a man is sexually aroused, this is the first gland to function. It sends a few drops of slippery neutralizing fluid into the urethra which prepares it for the safe passage of sperm, neutralizing the acids of the urine that would otherwise kill the sperm.

URETHRA—the tube which carries urine from the bladder through the penis in the act of liquid elimination. It also carries the sperm and semen from the prostate gland through the penis.

PENIS—the male sex organ through which both the urine and sperm are released. Under usual conditions the penis is very soft, spongy, and limpid. Under sexual arousement it is pumped with a large amount of blood which causes pressure, producing an erection which stretches the skin tight and makes the organ stand out from the body at an upward angle.

GLANS PENIS—the head of the penis, the very sensitive part of the organ which under friction produces an ejaculation of sperm and seminal fluid.

FORESKIN—the loose skin which covers the glans penis for protection. In more modern times when men wear clothes, it has been the custom to circumcise, or cut away, this skin during infancy for hygienic purposes. A substance called smegma often gathers under that foreskin, producing an offensive odor. For this reason the penis should be washed daily.

AREAS OF SEXUAL SENSITIVITY—the male genital organs, consisting of the penis, the scrotal sac and the area around them, are exceptionally sensitive to touch. When caressed affection-ately by the wife they produce a pleasurable sexual excite-ment that prepares the husband for the marriage act in a very few moments.

NOCTURNAL EMISSION (wet dream)—an unsettling experience to a boy unprepared for it. If he awakens to find his pajamas wet and sticky, or hardened to a starchy consistency he may be unnecessarily alarmed. What has happened is that pres-sure is built up by the phenomenal rate at which sperm are manufactured by the testicles until they become sensitive and swollen. The seminal vesicles are filled to capacity with fluid, as is the prostate gland, so that this entire reproductive system is waiting for an explosion. Sometimes a dream during the night will cause the penis to fill with blood, producing an erection. Cowper's gland puts forth its neutralizing drops of fluid into the urethra and then the ejaculatory muscles, or ducts, and the sperm and seminal fluids are merged and spurt forth through the urethra and the penis. Throughout a boy's teen years there will be many such nocturnal explosions. This constant production of sperm and seminal fluid causes the man to be the aggressor in initiating the act of marriage. His aggressiveness should not be looked upon merely as a means of satisfying the male sex urge, but as the fulfillment of the God-ordained plan of mutual sexual fellowship between a husband and wife.

The female reproductive system reveals the ingenious creative hand of God. The female organs are similar and complementary to the male reproductive system. This unique design will be revealed as you study the following organs and their functions.

THE FEMALE REPRODUCTIVE ORGANS [3]

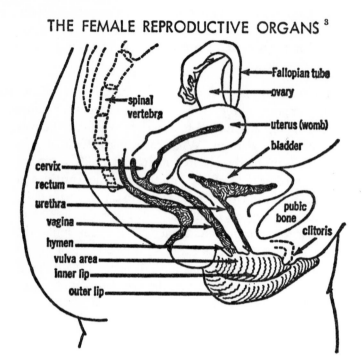

OVARIES—A woman has two ovaries, one on each side of her abdomen, located between her hip bones. These ovaries correspond to the male testicles and produce the female egg. When a girl is born, her ovaries contain thousands of little eggs called ova. After a girl matures, her ovaries begin to secrete the female sex hormones which cause her to develop. Her breasts begin to enlarge, hair grows under her arms and on her genital organs. Her hips begin to broaden, and she begins to take on a curvaceous, feminine appearance. At

[3]Joseph B. Henry, FULFILLMENT IN MARRIAGE (Westwood, New Jersey, Fleming H. Revell Company, 1966), p. 145. Used by permission.

approximately one month intervals one of her eggs matures until it is about one two-hundredths of an inch in diameter, at which time it is released by the ovary into the Fallopian tube.

FALLOPIAN TUBES—the tube attached to the ovary which takes the egg to the uterus during a period of approximately seventy-two hours. If intercourse is accomplished during this period, it is quite probable that at least one of the active sperm will work its way through the vagina and uterus into the Fallopian tubes and will unite with the egg. At that moment life is conceived. If the egg is not fertilized by the sperm in the Fallopian tube, it then passes into the uterus and dissolves.

UTERUS or WOMB—the area in which the baby grows during pregnancy. This pear-shaped organ can be greatly expanded.

VAGINA—the primary female sex organ comparable to the male penis and designed to receive it. It is made of soft, muscular tissue and provides a passageway from the outside of the body to the uterus.

VULVA AREA—the external opening to the vagina containing several organs, including the outer lips called "labia majora." These lips are formed from the same kind of coarse skin as the scrotal sac of the male. Under sexual excitement these lips swell or thicken. When these outer lips are opened, they reveal the inner lips called "labia minora," which are very delicate membranes at the front of the vulva structure. These inner lips are made of skin very similar to the skin of the glans penis.

HYMEN—the thin membrane characteristic of a virgin that makes deep penetration of the vagina by the penis difficult or sometimes impossible. Before marriage every young woman should be examined by a doctor; at his discretion, with her consent, the hymen can be broken to avoid unnecessary delay in intercourse after the wedding. If the young woman has serious objections to this procedure, a physical examination can be scheduled for the day after the wedding. Sometimes an over-anxious bridegroom can produce physical pain because of the presence of the hymen. Although this does not produce lasting damage physically, it can leave psychological scars if the bride associates pain with the entrance of the penis into the vagina. In this case, her fear will shut off the natural flow of body fluids in the vaginal area and cause painful intercourse that is most unsatisfactory to both partners.

CLITORIS—a small organ just above the urethra near the entrance to the vagina. It is usually encased within the vulva skin and is similar in structure to the male penis. When sexually aroused the clitoris will become firm and erect and be sensitive to touch or body contact. It is the manipulation of this organ by contact with the male penis, or man's body, that produces the female orgasm. There are two classes of female orgasms: clitoral and vaginal.

AREAS OF SENSITIVITY—A woman has more sensitive areas of sexual arousement than a man. This is probably God's means of compensating for the fact that the husband is ordinarily the initiator of the act of marriage. Because a woman's breasts are very sensitive, affectionate caressing helps to prepare her for the act of marriage. When aroused, her nipples will often become hard and protrude slightly, indicating proper stimulation. The large outer lips of the vulva area also become increasingly sensitive as they enlarge under arousement. The vagina and particularly the clitoris are also areas of sensitivity. When a woman is sexually aroused, several of her glands begin to secrete a lubrication that bathes the vulva area and the vagina with a slippery mucous, easing the entrance of the penis into the vagina. This has nothing to do with fertility, but is God's ingenious design for making the entrance of the dry penis a pleasurable experience to both the husband and the wife.

ORGASM—The climax of a woman's emotional stimulus in the act of marriage is followed by a gradual decline in sexual stimulation, producing a warm sense of gratification and satisfaction. A woman never ejaculates or expels fluid as does a man. Instead, he is the instigator and she is the receiver, not only of the male organ, but also of the sperm. Although not the titanic explosion-like experience of the male, the female's orgasm is just as gratifying, and some female psychologists have suggested it is even more so.

ATTITUDE

This explanation of the male and female reproductive organs prepares us for a discussion of attitude. One authority has stated, "Sex education is twenty percent education and eighty percent attitude." The right attitude is important for both husband and wife. The first thing to recognize is that the act of marriage (technically called *coitus*) is good. It was designed by God for man's good. It could well be described as the most sublime expression of love between two people when limited to the bonds of marriage. Because of the fact that taboos are properly put on the act of marriage during the teen-age and courtship years, Christian girls sometimes hesitate to enter enthusiastically into the relationship after marriage. Sometimes, because of preconceived ideas and false suggestions conveying an evil connotation, there is a subconscious association of guilt in fulfilling the act. Occasionally, a girl's viewpoint has been warped by a frustrated mother or grandmother whose sex life was unhappy, and she may secretly carry a feeling of dread to her marriage bed. These attitudes are contrary to God's plan:

> Marriage is honorable in all, and the bed undefiled: but whoremongers and adulterers God will judge (Hebrews 13:4).

> Let the husband render unto the wife due benevolence: and likewise also the wife unto the husband. The wife hath not power of her own body, but the husband: and likewise also the husband hath not power of his own body, but the wife. Defraud ye not one the other, except it be with consent for a time, that ye may give yourselves to fasting and prayer; and come together again, that Satan tempt you not for your incontinency (I Corinthians 7:3-5).

> So God created man in his own image, in the image of God created he him; male and female created he them. And God blessed them, and God said unto them, Be fruitful, and multiply, and replenish the earth, and subdue it: and have dominion over the fish of the sea, and over the fowl of the air, and over every living thing that moveth upon the earth (Genesis 1:27-28).

It is evident from these Scripture passages that the only taboos in the sex relationship are outside the bonds of marriage. That there is absolutely no connotation of evil involved in a proper relationship is seen in Genesis 1:28, where God commanded Adam and Eve to bring forth children. This command was given before sin reared its ugly head (Genesis, chapter 3).

Happy is the woman who looks upon the act of marriage as a means of showing her love for her husband and of his showing his love for her. In a vital sense it may be the only single experience she and her husband have together in which they do not have to share each other with another person. If she is a good cook, her husband may have to share her culinary arts with friends. If he is a good story teller, she also must share this ability with their friends. The same goes for their appearance, their manners, their courtesies, and practically every other area of life. The act of marriage, however, is unique in that it is the one experience from which they exclude the rest of the world.

Emotional Differences

The difference between the reproductive system of the husband and wife should stand as a symbol of the beautiful difference in their emotional make-up. Failure to understand this difference, particularly on the part of the man, will prevent the complete satisfaction that God intended intercourse to give to both the husband and wife.

The sex drive in a man is almost volcanic in its latent ability to erupt at the slightest provocation. Unlike a woman, a man is stimulated by sight. It was no accident that in Matthew 5:28 the Lord said of the man, "But I say unto you, That whosoever looketh on a woman to lust after her hath committed adultery with her already in his heart." He made no such statement concerning a woman. The reason is clear. Most women do not have the problem of looking at a man and lusting after him. Any army barracks will reveal that

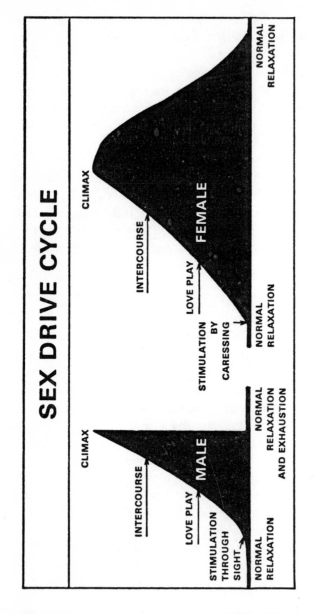

men are stimulated by sight, as exhibited by the pin-up pictures of scantily clad or nude women tacked on the walls. I have never heard of a woman who had pin-up pictures of nude men. It is the man who is stimulated by sight.

A woman responds to kind words and acts and a tender touch. A man, too, responds to touch, but not as completely as a woman does. A woman's emotions are less eruptive than a man's, but in the long run are just as electrifying. Her emotions have the ability to burn longer and go through a peak more gradually, even to the point of falling away more slowly.

The diagram on page 64 will give you an idea of the emotional difference and yet the equal satisfaction of both the husband and wife.

This stimulation difference can be illustrated by the simple procedure that takes place in many homes every night. A man watching his wife undress can be ready for the act of marriage before they get into bed. The wife, however, not being stimulated by sight, is only ready to go to bed. Unless the husband recognizes this emotional difference, their relationship will be fraught with many unsatisfying and maladjusted experiences. Unless he is willing to tenderly and affectionately express his love in an unselfish way, and through tender caressing give her emotions an opportunity to catch up to his, he will not be fulfilling the golden rule of marriage which is found in Philippians 2:3: "let each esteem other better than themselves."

A Personal Note To Husbands

There are several things you as a husband should remember. One is that you must learn self-control in an effort to make your marriage relationship truly meaningful and enriched. You can receive physical satisfaction in marriage very simply. But if at the same time your wife does not experience satisfaction, then your marriage under God will not reach its maximum potential. Carefuly consider these following suggestions.

• Women respond to tender affection and kind words. Begin your love play when you come home from work by greeting your wife with an affectionate kiss. With several expressions of affection throughout the evening, your wife will be more prepared for the act of marriage when you go to bed.

• Observe daily hygiene habits and by use of good deodorants keep down objectionable body odor.

• Remember that you should be the initiator because of your stronger sex drive. Ordinarily the wife will not initiate intercourse except possibly in the middle of the month, during the period of her fertility, or just before or after her menstrual period when her sex drive is particularly increased. Occasionally some women have stronger sex drives than their husbands; although this is not common, no faithful wife should associate such a drive with evil. Kept within the bonds of marriage, this can be a rich blessing, since it is usually easier for a woman to inspire a man to the marriage act than vice versa.

• Refrain from the use of back-alley words and expressions that associate evil with the act of marriage. Always refer to it with wholesome and endearing terms; thus, you will elevate it to the high and lofty heights that God intended for this sacred act.

• Seek to bring your wife to an orgasm in the act of marriage rather than just fulfilling your own desires. As you satisfy her, you will create in her a greater desire for the relationship; and thus, by giving love you will have your love returned.

- After the thrilling consummation of the act of marriage, don't be in a hurry to withdraw from your wife. Part of the satisfying effect for her is the physical closeness with her husband after their climax. Although it is more naturally appreciated by the wife, the husband can gradually learn to enjoy prolonging the experience.

- Maintain good lines of communication with your wife so that you can talk freely about these delicate matters. Frank communication about what is most enjoyable to your partner will help you both toward a good physical adjustment.

A Personal Note To Wives

Your attitude toward the act of marriage is one of the keys that will unlock the door to marital happiness. It may surprise you to know that a poor mental attitude toward sex is the primary cause of frigidity among women. "According to Drs. Willy, Vander and Fisher, authors of the *Encyclopedia of Sex*, not more than one-half of all women experience during the sexual act 'voluptuous pleasure rising to the intensity of orgasm.' "[4] Dr. Frank S. Caprio, a psychiatrist, has said, "The vast amount of current literature in psychosomatic medicine has convinced the majority of gynecologists that frigidity for the most part is psychological in origin. Proof of this lies in the fact that psychoanalysts have been definitely able to cure women of their frigidity via psychotherapy. By a process of reeducation a woman can learn how to overcome the inhibitions that very often prevent her from achieving a sexual orgasm."[5]

[4] Caprio, Frank S., M.D., THE SEXUALLY ADEQUATE FEMALE, (Greenwich, Conn., Fawcett Publications), p. 61. Used by permission.
[5] Ibid, page 67.

67

Combining these quotations we can legitimately conclude that almost fifty percent of the married women in so-called "sexually enlightened America" are sexually frustrated without a physical reason. Two of my doctor friends have confirmed this conclusion and agree that a woman's attitude is the most important factor in producing a satisfying climax in the act of marriage. When a woman is frustrated in the act of marriage something is wrong. God meant it to be a *mutually* satisfying experience. To help you approach this very important and meaningful part of your marriage with the desire of being a warm and responsive partner, consider the following suggestions:

• Try to rid your mind of any preconceived prejudices or "old wives' tales" that tend to make you fear the act of marriage—or look on it as evil. Just because your mother or some other woman was not well-adjusted in the physical area of marriage is no reason you have to perpetuate her mistakes and resultant misery. Approach the act of marriage with pleasurable anticipation. God meant it to be good!

• Learn to make an exception to the wholesome standards of modesty and virtue which you have been taught. Your husband should be the only exception! But he is an exception. Pre-marital taboos sometimes are hard to forget, but with God's help you can forget them. When they are carried over toward your husband, they become a false standard of modesty. I Corinthians 7 makes it clear that you should give control of your body to your husband; therefore, do not be afraid to expose yourself to him. The more you can relax in his presence, the better you will adjust. This usually comes in time. Recently a woman told me that after eight years of marriage she had never undressed in front of her husband. This is false modesty.

• Daily bathing is highly recommended. Some authorities suggest that a tub bath is preferable since the vaginal lubricants of the female anatomy can give off an offensive odor.

• The role of a woman is to respond. Don't resent this role, but relax and respond to your husband's affectionate expressions of love. You can usually thoroughly enjoy the experience if you relax!

• Many a wife has gotten into the habit of stifling her husband's advances by a tired sigh or a bored indication that means, "I don't feel like it tonight." In so doing she cheats them both out of a satisfying experience. Most women will respond to their husbands' mood if they will relax and give themselves to their husbands. The wife's first reaction to her partner's ardor often has nothing to do with her final enjoyment because God has given her the capacity to respond to her husband—if she will just let herself. A full understanding of this feminine response will help a woman overcome her selfish tendency to think first of how she feels when her husband approaches her and, instead, cause her to think how she will feel if she will relax and give herself to him.

• Since fear of pregnancy keeps a woman from enjoying the act of marriage to its fullest extent, be sure to consult your doctor for a good birth control program if you decide to delay a family.

• Don't be alarmed if you do not experience an orgasm during each sexual union with your husband. However, many women who do not experience an orgasm could if they would practice the following suggestion. Since a man's climax is reached by the friction of the vagina against the glans penis, he is stimulated by his instinctive in and out motion. To retard this climax, the husband should stop his movement so

69

that his feeling of explosion will decline. If the wife remains immobile during this period, her emotions will also decline. But the clitoris, which is the primary area that excites the wife to climax, is responsive to movements other than the in and out motions. When her husband stops, by slightly rotating or moving her hips, she can maintain the movement of his body against her clitoris. She may then continue building toward her emotional peak while he is waiting for his emotions to decline. When he is able to resume his instinctive movements, they will be able to climb together to their respective emotional peaks. It may be necessary for the husband to stop several times while the wife continues her climb through this very slight rotation technique. Concentration and practice will help couples to emotionally "peak out" together, which is the ideal goal both should work toward.

Another thing women can do to help themselves reach a climax in the marriage act is to develop their vaginal muscles. As previously stated, a woman can experience a vaginal orgasm as well as a clitoris-produced climax. Actually the two should work together toward a climax. Since the muscles of the vagina, like other muscles of the human body, can be developed by exercise, a wife should attempt to tighten these muscles daily, both during intercourse and when lying in bed. Five to ten minutes of daily flexing and tightening these muscles strengthens them and increases the capacity for sexual stimulation, thus assisting her ability to reach an orgasm.

• Sometimes a wife finds that one or two days a month, according to her reproductive cycle, the things that ordinarily cause great emotional stimulus actually work in reverse. Instead of increasing her sexual ardor, they actually dispel it and, in some cases, make her irritable. Don't be deceitful during these occasions. Be frank with your husband and obey Ephesians 4:15 by "...speaking the truth in love." Sometimes it is best not to engage in marital relationships at all at this time; other times, by limiting your preliminary love play to kissing, your physical relations can be consummated. Although it will be a rewarding experience, you will not find it to be the exhilarating and exciting experience that it is on most occasions.

● Keep the lines of communication on these matters open between you and your husband so that there is no misunderstanding. Most natural differences can be ironed out and a happy physical adjustment effected if two people will talk frankly about them.

● If you find that the relationship becomes a chore without enjoyment or meaning, seek the advice of a Christian counselor. God has better things for you.

An evangelist friend of mine told me a story that shows our heavenly Father's interest in one couple's maladjusted physical relationship. While he was holding a week of meeting in a certain city, a young husband he had led to Christ some years before insisted he stay at their home. This man was very successful in the business world and well respected in the Christian community. His beautiful wife and two lovely children gave them the appearance of being the ideal couple. Little did the evangelist dream that these two wonderful people had such a serious problem.

After breakfast the first morning he casually said to the wife, "How are things going?" She turned from the sink where she was working and tearfully cried, "Oh Ken, I'm so miserable!" She then related how completely frustrated she was in their physical relationship because her dynamic husband approached her with the same overpowering enthusiasm that he did everything in life, and consequently she felt used rather than loved. She had been praying that God would somehow help them in their relationship.

That night as he was getting ready for bed, the minister stepped into the bathroom to brush his teeth. Since the bathroom was between the two bedrooms, without trying to eavesdrop he could clearly hear his friend perform what he called "making love to my wife." It was all over in three minutes! It was nothing more than physical satisfaction of the masculine mating urge.

The next morning the evangelist asked his friend to stay home from work, and they talked in the backyard for two hours. To his amazement, this college graduate who dearly loved his wife didn't even know anything was wrong. Neither of these young people had read a book on the subject of sex and they had never been given marriage counseling. When the preacher finished the long-overdue counseling session, the young man was heartbroken. He confessed his selfishness to God and asked for divine wisdom in being the kind of husband that God wanted him to be, one that "loved his wife as his own body."

Six months later the evangelist met this couple at a banquet. During the evening the wife turned to him and said, "I can't thank you enough for what you have done for us. Our whole marriage has been transformed." My friend told me, "the look of joy on her face reminded me again that God is interested in every area of the Christian's life, including the physical adjustment."

Christian couples can have the best possible physical relationship in marriage, in spite of the fact that they usually start out as complete novices. God is interested in every area of life, including this very important relationship. He can either guide you to the right book or the proper counselor. Remember, God considers the act of marriage as the supreme expression of love between two human beings.

Suggested additional readings:

Butterfield, Oliver M., *Sexual Harmony in Marriage*. New York, Emerson Books, 1953.

Henry, Joseph B., *Fulfillment in Marriage*. New Jersey, Revell Company, 1966.

Lewin, S. A., M.D., *Sex Without Fear*. New York, Medical Research Press, 1961.

Robinson, Marie N., *The Power of Sexual Surrender*. Doubleday & Company, Inc., Garden City, New York, 1959.

When a child basks in the security of his parents' love he gradually
develops a wholesome outlook toward life.

5/ADJUSTING TO CHILDREN

Your childhood influences your desire for children. If you enjoyed a good home life you probably look upon children as a blessing. If you had a wretched childhood you may not want children. However, I have seen many people who used their background as a stimulus to provide their children with something better than they had.

Temperament, rather than background, often plays a bigger part in determining a person's desire for children. Mr. and Mrs. Sanguine invariably want children; they love people. Mr. Choleric wants them because he needs someone to provide for, or children to keep his wife busy. Mr. and Mrs. Melancholy are so indecisive and perfectionist prone, they probably will not choose to have children. They are too self-occupied to let anyone else into their little world. Mr. and Mrs. Phlegmatic usually want children because they are basically friendly, good-natured folks who like to do the accepted thing. Mrs. Choleric is perhaps the least prone to want children of any temperament type. She is so busy bossing, leading, or producing she doesn't want to be encumbered by little folks.

Fortunately for humanity, until recently having children

was not a matter of choice, it was a natural product of marriage. But even today temperament is not a complete deterrent, because "opposites attract each other"; and consequently, one or the other wants children.

God has mercifully given babies an uncanny ability to work into almost any parent's heart and carve out a special place of love. Rare indeed is that parent who can look his infant in the face and say, "I wish you had never been born." Instead, many who hesitated on the threshold of parenthood have responded to the paternal instinct once their child drew his first breath. In this day when planning or delaying a family is being over-emphasized, too many young couples are likely to cheat themselves out of one of life's most enriching experiences: being parents.

CHILDREN: NOW OR LATER

The trend of indefinitely delaying a family is currently sweeping the United States. With the advent of "The Pill" and other scientific methods of birth control, "planned parenthood" has become a reality. The problem is, most couples feel they will wait until they can afford children before ordering them. As I mentioned when discussing financial adjustments, it is easy to fall into the rut of an exaggerated standard of living in the early days of marriage when both the husband and wife are working. Many men can never increase their earning power to equal their combined incomes—or if they do, it takes so many years that the wife is long past the flower of her childbearing age. Many times as I have talked with a couple about adoption, they have said, "We waited until we could afford children and now we can't have them." This "waiting until we could afford children" concerns me because often the waiting is caused by a selfish desire for a high standard of living. The couple never finds the joy and satisfaction from material things that they would have found in having children.

The Ideal Childbearing Age

The ideal childbearing age is extremely short and not necessarily parallel with today's customs. By the time a young woman finishes high school today she is about eighteen years old. Unless her prospective husband is several years older she will often wait one to four years for him to complete his education or learn a vocation. By then she has either learned a skill or received a degree and goes to work in order to buy furniture or save money for a down-payment on a new home. Under such circumstances she is often twenty-two to twenty-six by the time she is ready for children, and surprisingly enough, that is past the ideal childbearing age.

We have four children in our family and only the birth of our son Lee caused severe complications for my wife. After unusually long labor, the gynecologist x-rayed her to see if he should perform a Caesarean section. As he explained to me, "This baby probably weighs nine to ten pounds and that is what is holding things up."

"How can that be?" I asked. "Our first two children weighed more than that."

Then he said, "But your wife isn't as young as she used to be." I laughingly replied, "Doctor, she is only twenty-five years old. I thought it was easier after each child."

I shall never forget his reply. "You don't understand," he said. "Most women are physically prepared to have children when they approach twenty years of age. From then on their ability to bear diminishes each year."

If God designed the female anatomy to bear children in

the latter teen years, he must have intended that girls become wives and mothers early in life. It is our culture, not the will of God, that has complicated parenthood by making it economically necessary to put off having a family. On the other side of the ledger most women are not particularly interested in becoming mothers after they are thirty-five or so years of age. I think we can reasonably conclude that the current average age for motherhood is somewhere between twenty and thirty-five with a tendency toward shortening the time even more.

Adoption

I want to briefly mention adoption. Because of modern pressures on women, and various other factors, an increasing number of childless Christian couples are confronted with the question: Should we adopt children or wait on the Lord to send them? Because of the moral breakdown of our day there seems to be more available children than parents.

Some couples have strange notions that children born out of wedlock are not likely to turn out as well as other children. That certainly has not been the case of adopted children within the range of my counseling experience. In fact, I have observed that parents who adopt children often want them more than natural parents want their children and consequently shower them with more love. To me, Christians adopting an illegitimate child is an almost certain method of evangelism. What started out as a tragedy can, by the grace of God and the unselfish love of a Christian couple, save a life as well as a soul.

REARING CHILDREN

What are the qualifications of a good parent? You do

not have to be a college graduate, for history reveals some of the greatest men had unlettered parents. It doesn't take riches, or charm, or natural gifts. I can sum up the requirements for parenthood in one word—maturity. Any young couple mature enough to live unselfishly with each other is qualified to be parents. Selfishness, the destroyer of marriage, is also devastating to children. All children need unselfish parents! The parents' adjustments as to whose responsibility it is to get up at night, whose responsibility it is to change the diapers, etc., can easily be set when approached with love and unselfishness.

I do not pretend to be an authority on rearing children and I cannot give detailed instruction, but three basic areas of responsibility that I want to present are: love, discipline, and training. Although they are inseparable and should be administered jointly, I shall discuss them separately.

Love

Nearly all psychologists and child specialists agree that the need for love in every human being is basic to proper development. A parent's love is more important to a child than wealth or education or any form of material possession. When a child basks in the security of his parents' love he gradually develops a wholesome outlook toward life. The home can fall far short of perfection in many areas; this lack will serve to prepare the child for life in an imperfect world. But the one thing he must have for a positive mental attitude is love.

For this reason parents must be careful to show love even as they administer corrective discipline. Overly critical, domineering parents produce fear-prone children. Even the most strong-willed child can be made indecisive if he is constantly harassed, criticized, and brow-beaten by his parents. Perfectionist-prone parents must be careful not to foist their perfectionist standards on their children, but to make them feel securely loved. A thoughtful parent can convey the thought to his child that although he does not approve of a particular action he nonetheless approves of him and loves him. After all, loving correction is the way our heavenly Father treats us: "whom he loveth, he chasteneth..." (Hebrews 12:6).

A minister friend of mine had a third child with a bed-wetting problem. While discussing the problem with the family doctor he was told that it was the result of a basic feeling of insecurity on the part of the child because he couldn't compete with his older brother and sister; thus, he felt inadequate and unloved. When the fourth baby was born she received the limelight that families naturally give to babies. This further convinced the boy that he was not loved as much as the other children.

The doctor suggested a plan which the father decided to follow. Each night before he went to bed he awakened the child and put him on the toilet. Then when he returned to bed in that semi-state of slumber the father took a few minutes to assure the child of his love and express genuine affection for the boy. He also gave positive suggestions of how important he was to the family and that in the morning he would be aroused by the desire to go to the bathroom and would instantly arise and go. Within two weeks the boy had some nights of success, and within two months, the father told me, the boy's problem was cured.

More important than curing the bed-wetting, the father reported, was the remarkable change in his son's attitude. He became a better student at school, his tendency toward rebellion and disobedience to gain attention was measurably decreased and a genuine spirit of affection grew between the father and his son. As the father continued to tell his son that he loved him, the son's subconscious mind finally received what every human being craves—the assurance of being loved.

Cannot Give Too Much Love

The one thing that we cannot give too much of to our children is love. Children need to be reassured by their parents of their love but then, isn't that also true of husbands and wives? Even after many years of marriage don't you still enjoy hearing those magic words from your partner, "I love you!" Fathers should be particularly careful to shower their daughters with affection. Most men do not realize the importance of extending this affection to their girls. The serious consequence of an inadequate father-daughter relationship was impressed upon me about nine years ago while talking with my wife's gynecologist who is a member of our church and a personal friend. We both do a lot of counseling so I asked him about a problem that was on my mind: "Has medical science come up with a pill that will cure frigidity?" He laughed and said, "Not to my knowledge!" He then added, "The best preventive medicine for that problem that I know of is an affectionate father."

Since then when counseling women who have a frigidity problem I have inquired about their relationship with their father and without exception it has been one of rejection since earliest childhood. Another possible cause of frigidity can be a traumatic experience such as child molestation that leaves an emotional fear-scar that prevents the girl from feeling relaxed in the presence of her husband. But even this tragedy has been overcome in some girls because they were fortunate enough to have had a very affectionate relationship with their father.

Transferral Of Love

It seems that when a little girl comes to her dad to be loved and is rejected, this rejection makes a lasting scar upon her subconscious mind. If her father never has time for her, never is interested in her little drawings, or does not let her sit on his lap or feel free enough to put her arms around his neck then in all probability she will develop a protective resistance to her father's rejection to avoid being continually hurt.

Since her first masculine image is her father she is prone to transfer this image to all men, including her husband. Whatever resentment and hostility she had been fostering in her heart against her father is often transferred to her husband. This faulty, but natural, conditioning process will prepare a girl for a less than ideal marriage and can be avoided by a thoughtful father who recognizes that every little girl needs to be loved by the one man in her life who is most important to her, her dad.

All of this talk about father-daughter affection does not mean that little boys are not also in need of love from their fathers and mothers. The above analysis simply illustrates one of the sad consequences of the lack of love. Many abnormal actions on the part of today's adults can be traced to the simple fact that as a child they were never assured of their mother's or father's love throughout their childhood. Fortunately, this devastating blow to a man's or woman's emotional nature can be cured by the power of Jesus Christ. God in his marvelous grace offers us the Holy Spirit to supply the peace, joy, love, and faith that every human being needs to have an adequate feeling of security, regardless of whether or not his parents loved him. But until a person goes to the Holy Spirit for help he will experience many unnecessary fears, doubts, and limitations because he didn't receive the love he needed.

Some parents more than others have to work on the matter of expressing their love because of their natural temperament and childhood experiences. A father I know committed what I considered a terrible blunder one day. His thirteen-year-old daughter skipped up to him in the exuberant effervescence of youth and spontaneously reached out to kiss him. His involuntary reaction was to turn his lips away and she kissed him on the cheek. It just happened that when his face turned her eyes were looking straight into mine and I saw that momentary look of disappointment on her face.

Deciding that his daughter's emotional development was worth risking our friendship, I later talked to the father about this incident. Fortunately he took my suggestion the right way and admitted it was difficult for him to show affection, particularly if he thought anyone was going to observe. As gently as I could I pointed out that he was indulging in selfishness—that more important than his inhibition at publicly showing emotion was his daughter's development. By God's grace he has learned to express his love genuinely and tenderly and I am pleased to say his daughter today enjoys a warm, endearing relationship with him that is preparing her to be a good wife and mother.

In conclusion, any parent can show love if he is mature enough to think more about his child than himself.

Discipline

A Christian Education professor in one of the leading

Christian colleges of our country once made this statement at a Sunday School convention: "Fifty percent of a child's character and personality development are accomplished by the time he is three years of age, and seventy-five percent by the time he is five years of age." Another speaker stated, "Show me a willful, rebellious, disobedient child of five and in ten years I will show you a willful, rebellious teen-ager. The time to bring teen-agers into control is before they are school age." These statements make it clear that the discipline of children should begin early in life. Sometimes I meet a parent who weakly says, "I love my children too much to spank them." That is not true; that is maudlin sentimentality. One of the most difficult things for a parent to do is to discipline his children. But it must be done!

Atheistic psychologists of thirty years ago started a snowball of ideas about parents' indulging their children that has caused much heartache today. Many modern teen-agers are victims of such ideas as the one my psychology professor shared with our class: "Spanking is old-fashioned and inhibits a child's development. Every child needs to learn to express himself." I am grateful that in addition to the psychology textbook I also had the Word of God that states, "he that spareth his rod hateth his son" (Proverbs 13:24).

Doing and Not Doing

One of the difficulties with current society is that too few people have been taught that some things in life cannot be done: One man cannot have absolute liberty without infringing on the rights of others. The best place for a child to learn that he must do some things in contrast to some other things he is forbidden to do is the home in which he is surrounded by love. That does not mean that spanking is the only means of discipline. Like most parents, in our youthful ignorance we probably spanked our first child more than the other three combined. As we grew up, however, we learned that there were other ways of using discipline that were equally effective—from sitting on the bed ten to thirty minutes depending on the crime, to taking away the keys to the family car.

One thing we as Christians should learn about administering discipline is that we never have to lose our temper and discipline our children in anger. Some parents tend to use spanking as a means of releasing their own pent-up anger and frustrations at a child's actions which happen to remind them of their own weaknesses. One of the most important things to remember in discipline is: consistency. Many parents end up spanking a child because they have been inconsistent. They will tell a child, "Now, Junior, don't do that" and forget that the minute they say "don't" Junior is going to put them to the test to see if they mean it. Because they fail the first test they say the same thing two or three times and then in exasperation resort to violence.

A good suggestion on discipline that will help avoid this inconsistency is: Don't forbid your child anything unless you really mean it. Then if he tests you, don't fail his test. We have found by trial and error what seemed to us to be a good method for those infractions of family rules which demanded spanking. We used a wooden spoon (probably because that was what I was reared on). The first time they did something that was forbidden, they got one spank with the spoon; for the second infraction they received two spanks; and for the third they received three, and so on. For some reason it was never necessary to give more than three for a given offense. The secret to this, or any form of discipline, is consistency.

Children quickly learn that parents have different ideas in certain areas of discipline. They immediately begin to exploit these differences by pitting one parent against another. The solution to this problem is like all the others—loving communication. Most couples do not establish set standards of behavior, but try to deal with every crisis when it comes. It is much better to set guidelines; children are more comfortable and discipline is more consistent. Both parents should agree that when one speaks, both have spoken; thus, they will avoid the dilemma of the child who disobeys dad with mother's permission. That does not mean you will always agree with your partner's interpretation of the rules. Your disagreement, however, should be reserved for your partner, in secret. If he agrees he has made a mistake, then he should be the one to change it. Most of the time you will find that it is more important for mother and dad to maintain unity before the children than to resolve the particular issue at hand.

Training

The best educational institution in the world is the home. Current society has defaulted on this opportunity and tries to make the school, television, and sometimes the church do its training. This shifting of responsibility is proving inadequate because the atheistic agitators in our country have caused the school administrators to be afraid to teach moral principles and standards of behavior. Television is more degrading than uplifting and too few of our children go faithfully to Sunday school.

Gain Early Rapport With Children

Most parents fail to realize the tremendous advantage they have with their children. In the early stages of life the words of a father are more significant to a boy than even the words of God. Unfortunately, too many fathers do not avail themselves of this precious opportunity. Fortunate indeed is the teen-ager who can naturally go to his father and/or mother for advice because this rapport was established in early childhood.

My wife and I were privileged to view this father-son relationship from an unusual vantage point. The Christian young man our daughter dated for most of her high school years had an ideal relationship to his father that influenced their courtship behavior. In fact, when my sixteen-year-old son started dating and it was time to have the traditional father-son talk I used this lad as a good example. When I told my son that his parents and his Lord expected him to treat every girl as a lady he knew what I meant for he had seen this young man treat his sister that way. When I told him we expected him to help every girl he dated to obey the rules her parents established, he knew by example what we meant. When I told him that by cooperating with both his parents and the girl's parents he could have happy and enjoyable teen years he understood because he had seen his sister and her boyfriend have a "ball" through high school. I furthermore emphasized that this standard of behavior was not put upon him because his parents were in the ministry, but because he was a Christian and that was the happiest way for him to live.

Unfortunately, many Christian fathers don't tell their sons these things, or else their sons don't listen. For I have learned from girls who come to me for counseling that many

Christian boys can't be trusted as much as some of the other boys. This is the result of faulty parental training.

Black and White—Or Gray?

Moral behavior standards are in a state of flux today. Contemporary Americans seem to think it is wrong to have blacks and whites, rights and wrongs. They tend to adopt the current relative standard of dumping all morals into a gray zone. Thinking of moral behavior in terms of gray, instead of black and white, causes people to put off making a decision until they are in the midst of a situation and forced to make a decision. Then people often regret these snap decisions. Living this way is frantic nonsense! It not only produces indecisive and emotionally unstable people, but it creates social havoc.

The Bible provides a standard of right and wrong. Instead of apologizing for it, we ought to teach it to our children "line upon line, precept upon precept." The Bible says, "Be not conformed to this world: but be ye transformed by the renewing of your mind, that ye may prove what is that good, and acceptable, and perfect, will of God" (Romans 12:2). If you want the perfect will of God for your children, then it is your responsibility to teach it to them.

Teen-age Rebellion

"What about teen-age rebellion?" Counselors are increasingly asked this question. Some strong-willed young people seem to go through an unusual streak of rebellion in their teen-age years, regardless how lovingly and carefully they were reared. This must be the group Dr. Henrietta Mears, an authority on Christian Education, referred to facetiously when she said, "Some teen-agers become so cantankerous only their mother and father can love them, and sometimes the father can't understand how the mother can put up with them."

High school is a difficult time for any young person because as an emerging adult he has many new opportunities and responsibilities, but often he does not have enough insight or experience on which to base decisions. He is frequently faced with crossroad situations. Which way is he going to take? Will he do this or that? Many of his decisions and actions at this time affect—either negatively or positively—his future.

Worrying about them at this stage certainly will not help. Try to understand the change and confusion they are going through. And commit them to God, trusting him as the Bible teaches in Psalm 37 to protect them through this tempestuous phase of life.

One of our close friends and his wife had a traumatic experience with their teen-age daughter who was going through a Beatle-worshiping phase. She and a friend from church secretly purchased tickets to a Beatle performance on a Sunday night during church time. In their excitement to see their idols neither of the girls thought of how they were going to get home after 10:00 p.m. forty miles across the city of Los Angeles.

The girls had saved for weeks for this event but neither said anything about her plans to her parents. About 4:00 p.m. on the day of the performance my friend's wife realized she did not know where her daughter was. Instinctively apprehensive, she went into her daughter's room and noticed an announcement of the event. Becoming suspicious she called the other girl's mother and found her daughter, too, was missing. As they talked about the situation, they were terrified by the realization that their daughters had willfully, defiantly, and with premeditation secretly gone to watch the Beatles. In a matter of minutes the parents met to decide what to do. My friend decided they needed divine counsel, so they prayed. At first the fathers thought they should go look for the girls, but my friend had the lead solo part in the church's choir concert beginning at seven o'clock that night. In fact, his wife and daughter were also scheduled to sing in the choir. As they looked to the Lord for guidance he decided that it was his responsibility to fulfill his planned obligation and trust God to let the other father find the teen-agers.

How does a father find two girls out of 60,000 teen-agers milling, screaming, and churning around? He spent almost an hour looking for them, and at the same time asked God to guide him. It was no coincidence that the girls went into a restaurant for a snack before going into the stadium and sat at a table in front of a large window facing the street. Neither was it a coincidence that the father looked into that window as he passed, and saw the girls. They didn't willingly come, but angrily and tearfully; he forced them into the car and drove home.

My friend's daughter came into the house screaming hysterically in a manner unique to frustrated teen-agers. Her mother gave her about ten minutes then made her dress for church. The mother insisted that her daughter go to church and take her place in the front row of the choir.

After the service her father explained to her that more than sinning against them (her parents) and herself, she had sinned against God in being disobedient. He then prayed for her and urged her to go and pray for herself and said, "I haven't made up my mind what your punishment is going to be, but I will let you know before the week is over." He decided that the price of her disobedience would be destruction of her Beatle records. She destroyed them with all the dignity of a melancholy funeral service.

Later, much to her parents' amazement she said, "As a Christian I really shouldn't listen to that kind of music anyway." The change in that girl from that point on has been almost unbelievable. The willful rebellion that was apparent to all who loved her has just faded away and she has become a lovely enjoyable person and has more friends. She is taking a position of leadership that has not only delighted her parents, but has also brought a great degree of satisfaction to herself.

Set Limits and Definite Rules

It isn't always easy to set limits and define rules to our children and teen-agers, but it certainly pays. Sometimes they argue and fight over the rules you establish while secretly appreciating them. I once heard a psychologist tell of a young girl who was brought to him by her parents because she wouldn't date. Counseling revealed she didn't know what was expected of her; consequently, she felt insecure and refused all invitations to go out.

God has given teen-agers parents, so that before they realize the power of the flesh and its natural deceitful lusts, guidelines and principles for their behavior can be set. Good training involves explanation and all rules should be clear, but with many teen-agers there comes a time when no amount of reasoning will make them joyfully accept their parents' decision. Don't be deterred by their objections, set good rules whether they like them or not. A good formula for parents to keep in mind when setting dating, or any other rules for children, is BOY + GIRL × OBEDIENCE TO GOD = HAPPINESS. The boy + girl part seems to come naturally.

The obedience to God factor of this equation is our responsibility as parents. It is by faith that we present these "old-fashioned" concepts and principles because we believe God's ways are best.

Like most pastors, I keep a file in my desk marked "Special Letters" but the one I treasure more than all the rest came from my eldest daughter, Linda, two weeks after she arrived at the university. The sentence she wrote that has burned its way into my heart is profoundly simple. She said, "And Dad, I want to thank you for being my father." That letter more than made up for those occasional tense moments when Dad and Linda did not see eye-to-eye because my "dating standards are old-fashioned" or "do I really have to be in by 11 o'clock?" or "why do we always have to double date?" or "what's wrong with that, all the other kids have gone?" Sure, I felt like an ogre, but I thank God that my wife and I stuck to our principles. Now Linda and I both know it was right, and I have a hunch someday she will set pretty much the same standards for my grandchildren.

Be Your Child's Example

One final but very important aspect of parental training should not be overlooked. That is, the aspect of training by example. The old adage of "what you do speaks so loud I can't hear what you say" is never more true than in the parent-child relationship. The best sermons your children will ever hear are the ones they see you live. You may regularly attend a church that has the greatest preacher in the world, but if you do not live a Christ-like life before your children most of what your pastor preaches is nullified by your behavior. The Bible teaches: "be thou an example of the believers." This command is particularly appropriate for parents. It is one thing to act like a Christian on Sunday; it is another thing to be a Christian at home. Any man that is a real Christian in the eyes of his family, is a real Christian. Christian parents should adopt the standard of behavior set by the Apostle Paul when he said to his spiritual sons and daughters, "be ye followers of me, even as I also am of Christ." When life is over and we look back, the greatest joy that can fill our hearts is to be able to say with the Apostle John, "I have no greater joy than to hear that my children walk in truth" (3 John 4).

Special Responsibility

Too frequently, parents take their child's salvation for granted. Recently the wife of a Christian worker came to me to say that even though reared in a Christian home she had never personally invited Jesus Christ into her life. She knew about him, she believed in him, but she had never been "born again." Her parents just took it for granted that she was a Christian and when she timidly tried to hint that she wasn't they ridiculed the idea and frightened her out of making a clear-cut decision. Fortunately, her husband had better judgment than her parents and when she confronted him with the fact he graciously understoood and led her to Christ. This young lady's frustrations could have been easily avoided by thoughtful parents. Since we have a special place in the child's heart, we have a special responsibility to lead our children to Christ.

One Sunday morning a young dentist came to me at the close of the service and said, "Pastor, my son Casey is ready to receive Christ. Would you talk to him, please?" I said, "Ron, as much as I enjoy leading people to Christ I wouldn't cheat you out of that blessing. Go home and explain to him how to receive Jesus. If he doesn't, then I will be glad to talk to him." I shall never forget the exuberant joy with which that father greeted me that Sunday night as he told how Casey had very simply invited the Savior into his life. Don't wait for someone else to lead your children to Christ, but trust God to use you— the dearest friend they have on this earth—to lead them to the Savior.

1. Unless the Lord builds a house, the builders' work is useless. Unless the Lord protects a city, sentries do no good.

2. It is senseless for you to work so hard from early morning until late at night, fearing you will starve to death; for God wants His loved ones to get their proper rest.

3. Children are a gift from God; they are His reward.

4. Children born to a young man are like sharp arrows to defend him.

5. Happy is the man who has his quiver full of them. That man shall have the help he needs when arguing with his enemies* (Psalm 127, *Living Psalms and Proverbs*).

---

*Literally, "When they speak with their enemies in the gate."

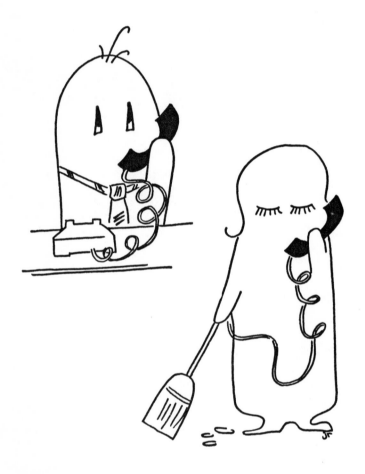

The way to have something is to give it away. If you want love, for example, don't look for it—give it.

6/SIX KEYS TO MARITAL HAPPINESS

Many a time I have wished I were a magician! When a married couple tells me their problems and resultant miseries, I would love to wave a magic wand over them and watch them leave my office to "live happily ever after."

Naturally, I don't have such a wand. But I do have six keys that are guaranteed to open the door to a happy marriage. Examine each key carefully. The degree to which you use them determines the success of your marriage. If you neglect them, your marriage cannot help but be a miserable and wretched experience. These keys come from the Bible, God's manual on human behavior. Therefore, I can guarantee happiness and success to all who use them.

MATURITY

The first key that guarantees happiness in marriage is *maturity*. This key is best defined in the emotional realm as unselfishness. Babies and small children are selfish—thus we refer to them as immature. When a child throws a fit in a supermarket by lying on the floor, screaming, and kicking his feet because he can't have his way, he is revealing his selfishness or immaturity.

If such a child is not properly disciplined, he will go into marriage so immature that he will want his own way in practically every situation. Such an attitude, very subtle and difficult for the immature person to recognize, is disastrous to a marriage.

The Problem

The adjustment stage of marriage, usually considered the first three years, will naturally produce conflicts of interest. For the first twenty or more years of their lives people function as independent gears. They make decisions purely on the basis of what they want or what is good for them. After the wedding, two independent individuals must learn to mesh together. Since they are both moving objects, and all movement creates friction, there is bound to be friction as they learn to move together in unity.

This friction is illustrated in the old-fashioned transmission. As long as the car stands still without the motor running, you can move the gear shift, meshing different gears at will, without problems. Once in motion, it is quite a different matter. It is not uncommon to hear these moving gears "clash" as the car is shifted in an effort to increase its speed. Automobile manufacturers solved this problem in recent years by installing a "synchromesh gear." This gear makes possible the bringing together of two or more moving gears in unity without "clashing."

The *synchromesh gear* in marriage is *unselfishness.* If two mature people come together in marriage, their spirit of selflessness will make it very easy for them to adjust. If they are immature and selfish, the early years of their marriage will be filled with "noisy clashes."

Marriage consists of a series of actions and reactions motivated by our conscious and subconscious minds. The more active the people, the more potential areas of conflict can be expected. Conflict, however, need not be fatal. In fact, some counselors suggest that conflicts are normal and can provide a creative force in marriage. Dr. Alfred B. Messer, addressing the American Psychiatric Convention in October of 1966, said, "A spirited spat is good for most marriages... Arguments are inevitable in a marriage and probably offer one of the best ways couples have to work out touchy problems. When most of the frustrations have been talked out or discharged in some vicarious way, the fight can be ended. Those marriages that exist without any type of fighting are generally frozen or inflexible marriages in which other aspects of the relationship are compromised in order to maintain the facade of peace and harmony."

Although some conflict is inevitable between two normal human beings, fighting is not necessarily the answer. By God's grace, two mature people can face their areas of conflict, discuss them, and by obeying the injunctions of God's Word resolve them. Don't get into the habit of sweeping your problems under the rug. Face them and resolve them in the SPIRIT. Actually, there is nothing wrong with having a conflict of interest between husband and wife. In fact, every such case is a test of your maturity. The partner that demands "his own way" in such conflicts is traveling a collision course that will produce much unhappiness for both of them.

You Never Get By Getting

After I completed a marriage counseling session some

years ago, the prospective bride looked at me and said, "Your advice is sure different from the advice the girls at the office gave me. They said, 'Bonnie, one thing to remember in marriage is that men are out for all they can get. Don't give too much of yourself to your husband; he'll just take advantage of you.'" That unchristian and unsound attitude is one of the things that produces so much misery in American homes.

In God's economy, you never get anything by getting. The way to have something is to give it away. If you want love, for example, don't look for it—give it. If you want friends, don't look for friends—be friendly. The same is true of thoughtfulness, consideration and selflessness. If you want your partner to treat you unselfishly, then be mature enough by God's grace to treat him unselfishly.

Why did you get married in the first place? The answer to that question may give you an insight into your maturity. Did you get married because "I had an unhappy home life" or because "I got tired of my parents' telling me what to do" or because "All of my friends were getting married and I didn't want to be left alone" or because "I wanted somebody to love me"? The proper attitude that guarantees success in a marriage is based on mature unselfishness. Mature individuals will go into marriage not only for what they can get out of it, but for what they can give to their partners. Two verses in the Bible come close to being a magic wand; when used by marriage partners, they turn chaos into peace and harmony:

> Let nothing be done through strife or vainglory; but in lowliness of mind let each esteem other better than themselves. Look not every man on his own things, but every man also on the things of others (Philippians 2:3-4).

If you go into marriage with this attitude—"look not on your own things...but on the things of your partner"—you will discover happiness in your home. Your attitude should never be that it is your partner's responsibility to make you happy. You must initially recognize your responsibility to make your partner happy.

There is an irrelevant and erroneous saying about marriage that has somehow become popular: Marriage is a fifty-fifty proposition. Nothing could be further from the truth! Marriage, under God, should be a one hundred percent to nothing proposition. That is, you should go into your marriage with the idea that you are going to give yourself for the purpose of making your partner happy and expect nothing in return. The result will be your own happiness. Your desire in marriage should be to make your partner happy. Of course, if you do that you will reap happiness in return.

A sharp young couple came to see me some years ago with conflict written all over their marriage. George had come from a very secure home. His greatest pleasure was to go hunting with his father on weekends. Ellen came from a very insecure home where her parents' many conflicts produced an early desire for her to get married and get away from it all. After four years of marriage they had discovered that their love was not destroyed, but they were at such cross purposes that they knew that it soon would be if something were not done.

I soon discovered that they both were disappointed in the results of their marriage. They had entirely different concepts of married life. Ellen, who was inclined to escape the nasty realities of now by dreaming about an Utopian future, wanted marriage to be a "blissful time of relaxation and family life, particularly on weekends." George thought marriage should be a relaxed home life five nights a week, with most weekends spent hunting and fishing with his father and some day, he hoped, with his son. In fact, he wanted to get married as soon as he did because he spent so much time with Ellen while courting her that he had to give up some of his treasured hunting experiences.

Strangely enough, they both knew what the problem was; they just had never faced it before. Every time he planned a trip with his father, Ellen would become angry and they would exchange cutting remarks. When she crawled into her self-protective shell of silence and frigidity, it was even worse. Sometimes he couldn't enjoy the hunting trip because he knew things were not right at home.

Fortunately, these two people were mature enough to face the fact that their marriage was more important than "togetherness" or hunting trips. We worked out an agreement in which they would both give in to the other's desires on this matter. George went on only half as many hunting trips and Ellen tried hard to send him out of town in a good spirit. Several times she didn't feel very good about it, but for his sake she tried vigorously and succeeded.

Then one day a friend invited them to go water skiing. Both were excellent swimmers, and they took to this form of entertainment like ducks take to water. A few weeks later they bought a boat and now regularly go out on Saturdays with friends for an enjoyable time together.

Was it a great sacrifice for George? When I asked him some months later how things were going, he replied, "For some reason I've lost a lot of my interest in hunting and fishing. I only go three or four times a year now. I would rather go water skiing with Ellen, or do something else with her and the children." Don't be afraid of giving in. All you will do is win in the long run.

Selfishness Is Universal

Selfishness, the greatest single enemy to a happy marriage, is a basic part of man's fallen nature. All temperaments have one thing in common: the weakness of selfishness. This selfishness is revealed differently in each temperament. For example, the strong extrovert Mr. Sanguine reveals his selfishness in egotism and angry impatience toward others. The moderate extrovert Mr. Choleric exhibits his selfishness in an angry and cruel disregard for the feelings of others. Mr. Melancholy displays his selfishness through self-centered introspection that produces fear and indecision. The quiet and easygoing Mr. Phlegmatic reveals his selfishness in his stubborn refusal to get involved with the problems of others lest he be hurt. Consequently, he is usually a fearful person.

The important thing to remember is that something can be done to overcome selfishness. The Bible tells us in 2 Corinthians 5:17, "Therefore if any man be in Christ, he is a new creature: old things are passed away; behold, all things are become new." The Greek construction of this verse indicates the gradual passing away of old things, which includes man's natural selfishness. When Jesus Christ comes to live in a person's life, he creates a new nature within him that, if yielded to and nurtured, will overpower the old nature.

How To Overcome Selfishness

Selfishness can be corrected by the power of God in conjunction with a cooperative individual. God will give you the power if you are willing to cooperate with him. The following steps are highly successful in changing selfish behavior into unselfish acts of thoughtfulness toward others.

• Face your selfishness as a sin! Until you are able to recognize your selfishness as a sin displeasing to God and to

103

others, you will never be able to think of others before you think of yourself. Too many people excuse it on the basis that "I was given a free hand by my parents and I just developed the habit of doing whatever I want." The fact that your parents made the mistake of indulging you by not limiting your activities to those areas that were good for you is no reason to perpetuate that mistake for a lifetime. Instead, face it as a sin.

• Don't try to hide behind academic or economic success to cover your selfishness. Maturity is relative. That is, a man may be a brilliant scientist and a good leader at work, but a selfish, overgrown baby as a husband at home. A woman may be an effective organizer and women's club president or church worker, but a selfish, childish, miserable wife. Face the truth that no matter what you are in the business or academic world, if you fail in your marriage, you have failed in an important area of your life. Selfishness is the greatest cause of marital failure.

Once you have faced the fact that your selfishness, regardless of your partner's behavior, is a sin before God, you have made a giant step. Before you will submit to an operation, your doctor must convince you that you have a disease or some other physical malady. Excusing the symptoms will never correct the problem. The same principle applies in the emotional realm. As long as you cover up your selfishness, excuse it, or ignore it, you will never correct it. Happy is the man who understands that he, and he alone before God, is responsible for his actions and reactions, and that when he acts with a selfish motive he has sinned against God as well as against his fellow man.

• Confess your selfishness as a sin. There are no big sins or little sins in God's sight. Sin is sin. Whenever you act selfishly, be sufficiently objective about yourself to confess your sin to your heavenly Father, then be assured that he will forgive you (I John 1:9).

• Ask God to take away the habit of being selfish. "And this is the confidence that we have in him, that, if we ask anything according to his will, he heareth us: And if we know that he hears us, whatsoever we ask, we know that we have the petitions that we desired of him" (1 John 5:14-15). Since it is not God's will that we be selfish creatures, he will direct us in changing our habit of behaving selfishly.

• Repair the damage done by your selfishness. Whether or not he deserves it, apologize to whomever you exhibited your immaturity or self-seeking and you will find it easier and easier to avoid selfish behavior. A person soon learns that he would rather not be selfish because it is harder to humble himself enough to say, "I was wrong. Will you forgive me?" than to give up selfish behavior!

• Repeat this formula every time you do or say something under the motivation of selfishness. It will help you become a happy, well-adjusted, and unselfish person whose company other people enjoy. In addition, your maturity may gradually inspire maturity in your partner. Before you realize it, the key of maturity will open many doors to happiness in your marriage.

SUBMISSION

No organization can function properly if it has two heads. That is particularly true of the home. One of the great hindrances to a happy home today is the false notion that a woman does not have to subject herself to her husband. Modern psychology and education seem to give women the idea that subjection is an old-fashioned notion that went out with the nineteenth century. But when subjection goes out of the home, so does happiness.

Today we have more frustrated women, men and children than ever before. With the downgrading of the father image and the rising dominance of the mother role we have witnessed an increase in juvenile delinquency, rebellion, homosexuality and divorce. God intended man to be the head of his home. If he is not, he will not have a sense of responsibility but will subconsciously feel he is married to a second mother. His children will soon detect who is boss, and as teen-agers they will lose the natural respect for their father that is necessary for their adjustment to life.

Usually a wife-dominated home is a quarrelsome home until the husband finally "gives up." He then crawls into his shell of introversion and degenerates into a sub-par human being. The sad thing is, a wife will eventually grow to despise the husband she dominates.

A Command Of God

The Christian woman must be in subjection to her husband! Whether she likes it or not, subjection is a command of God and her refusal to comply with this command is an act of disobedience. All disobedience is sin; therefore, she cannot expect the blessing of God on her life unless she is willing to obey God. The following Scripture passages establish this fact.

> Unto the woman he said, I will greatly multiply thy sorrow and thy conception; in sorrow thou shalt bring forth children; and thy desire shall be to thy husband, and he shall rule over thee (Genesis 3:16).

> Wives, submit yourselves unto your own husbands,

as unto the Lord. For the husband is the head of the wife, even as Christ is the head of the church: and he is the savior of the body.

Therefore as the church is subject unto Christ, so let the wives be to their own husbands in every thing (Ephesians 5:22-24).

...and the wife see that she reverence her husband (Ephesians 5:33).

Likewise, ye wives, be in subjection to your own husbands; that, if any obey not the word, they also may without the word be won by the conversation of the wives; While they behold your chaste conversation coupled with fear (I Peter 3:1-2).

The refusal of many Christian wives to accept the principle of subjection is increasingly common today. A number of years ago I taught a Bible class of forty-five adults—twenty-three women and twenty-two men. I gave the results of the curse of Genesis 3 on the man, the woman, and the ground and the serpent. Concerning the woman, I pointed out that she had two parts to her curse: one, sorrow in childbirth; two, being ruled over by her husband. The next week I gave an examination and believe it or not, in response to the question, What was the result of the curse to the woman? I received twenty-three female answers: She shall have sorrow in childbirth. The twenty-two men answered: She shall be ruled over by her husband. A few of the men also included that she would have sorrow in childbirth. The fact that not one of those twenty-three women, who voluntarily attended that Bible class for the purpose of spiritual growth, had remembered the subjection part of the curse illustrated to me the universal tendency of women to reject this God-given command.

107

God's Tool For Your Happiness

God never commands people to do that which is impossible or is not for their good. The Holy Spirit has asked in Romans 8:32, "He that spared not his own Son, but delivered him up for us all, how shall he not with him also freely give us all things?" The answer to that is, if God loved us so much that he gave his Son to die for us, certainly he will give us all those things that are for our good. Therefore, by faith accept the fact that submission to her husband is for a woman's good.

Somewhere between thirty-five and forty-five a woman usually reaches a period when she increasingly desires to become a leaner. If she is aggressive in the early years of marriage and dominates her husband, she teaches him to lean on her. Then, when she gets to the age where she wants a man to lean on, she finds that she has created a leaner and has no one on whom she can lean. I've seen many a woman at this stage come to loathe the man whom she, in her younger years, trained to be a docile, submissive spouse.

It is safe to assume that dominating wives have caused great misery in marriage, both to themselves and to their partners. The woman who enjoys bossing her husband when she is twenty-five may find life turning into a nightmare as she advances in age. It is an act of faith in a Christian woman's heart to assume that for her lasting happiness and of the happiness of her husband it is essential that she be obedient to God and put herself in subjection to her husband.

Subjection Is Not Slavery

When a Christian woman seeks God's grace and the filling of the Holy Spirit to enable her to live in subjection to her husband, she is not in danger of becoming a slave. Many times I have seen women seek to be subjected for spiritual reasons only to find that the reaction in their husband has been one of thoughtfulness and kindness which caused a cessation of hostilities between them. Usually a woman finds that she fares far better when she is in subjection than when she dominates. Certainly she will enjoy a better walk with God when she is obedient to her husband for the Lord's sake, than when she disobeys God by dominating her husband.

Subjection does not mean that a woman can't voice her opinion by "speaking the truth in love" (Ephesians 4:15), but that she should seek to be submissive to her husband's desires when he reaches a decision and that she comply with his requirements whenever humanly possible. There may be times when she will have to do something that she really doesn't want to do, but by sowing the seeds of obedience on that matter she will reap the harvest of blessing on many others. Always remember, you reap far more than you sow. If you sow submission in obedience to God, you will reap blessing in abundance; if you sow rebellion in disobedience to the will of God, you will reap abundant misery. Some women have a more aggressive temperament than their husbands and admittedly it is more difficult for them to be in subjection. In fact, the only way I know they can is to recognize that it is a spiritual responsibility. When this fact has been established in her mind, any woman can summon the grace of God to be the submissive person God wants her to be.

Some years ago I counseled with a woman who was far more aggressive than her husband and found that through the years even though he was well-educated she had made the major decisions of the family. He was an easygoing phlegmatic person and she was a combination of sanguine and choleric temperament. Thus, when children came in to ask questions he would be relaxed and quiet while she answered and made decisions. At about thirty-five years of age she recognized that he was gradually receding into a shell of compliance in the home and she was assuming dictatorial powers. When she became convinced of her need to submit to her husband for the Lord's sake she asked God to help her bite her tongue and stifle her intuitive inclination to make spontaneous decisions—and to wait for her husband to make the decision. She was amazed to find that in a brief period of time he rose to the challenge and gradually assumed the decision-making prerogatives in the home. Interesting to me as I counseled with this woman was the fact that the more she submitted, the more he led; the more he led, the happier he was; and the happier he was, the happier she was. That marriage was gradually changed from the point of living together because they were Christians to a new spark of genuine love and respect for each other. To me, this couple is a living example of the fact that a wife's submission to her husband is a key to a happy marriage.

LOVE

The third key that guarantees a happy marriage is *love*. Probably no other word is more misunderstood in the English language than this one. Most people today do not know what love is. They often confuse physical attraction, lust, personal desire, sympathy, or compassion with love. Love is one of the most common experiences of man and one of the most difficult to define. Webster defines it as "a feeling of strong personal attachment induced by sympathetic understanding, or by ties of kinship; ardent affection."

The Bible says the love of a husband for his wife should equal his love for himself. God instructed him to love his wife sacrificially as Christ loved the church and gave himself for her (the church). No woman can be unhappy when given that kind of love, and the husband that gives that kind of love will be the recipient of sacrificial love.

Like God, love cannot be seen, but we know of its existence because of its effects. It is easier to describe love than define it. Although many have attempted a description of love, in all the annals of literature there is none that compares with those masterful words that come from the pen of the apostle Paul in the great love chapter, 1 Corinthians 13. Note this beautiful description as it appears in the *Living New Testament* paraphrase by Kenneth Taylor (verses 4-7):

> Love is very patient and kind, never jealous or envious, never boastful or proud, never haughty or selfish or rude. Love does not demand its own way. It is not irritable or touchy. It does not hold grudges and will hardly even notice when others do it wrong. It is never glad about injustice, but rejoices whenever truth wins out. If you love someone you will be loyal to him no matter what the cost. You will always believe in him, always expect the best of him, and always stand your ground in defending him.

Henry Drummond, in a book entitled *The Greatest Thing in the World*, points out the nine characteristics of love found in this preceding passage: patience, kindness, generosity, humility, courtesy, unselfishness, good temper, guilelessness, and sincerity. Study these characteristics and examine your love to see if it meets God's standards of acceptable expression.

These nine characteristics or expressions of love communicate the love of one human being to another in terms that are meaningful to everyone, regardless of race or background. No one will naturally express his love in all of these characteristics. Some people are patient and kind by nature, but lack humility, generosity or confidence. Others are naturally sincere and courteous, but lack a good temper and are prone to be impatient. All men need the power of the Holy Spirit to supply the kind of love God expects us to extend to our partner. The Holy Spirit gives the Christian (Galatians 5:22-23) the ability to express complete love.

The love that God requires of a husband for his wife and wife for her husband is admittedly a supernatural love. Self-preservation is the first law of life; therefore, to love someone else as your own body demands a supernatural kind of love. It is just not possible for man to love this way of his own accord. However, since God never commands us to do that which he will not enable us to do, we can call upon him, the author of love, and know that he will supply us with that kind of supernatural love. The Bible tells us, "Beloved, let us love one another, for love is of God, and every one that loveth is born of God and knoweth God" (1 John 4:7).

Both husband and wife are commanded to love each other, but it should be pointed out that while the wife is commanded once (Titus 2:4) to love her husband, the husband is commanded at least three times to love his wife (Ephesians 5:25, 28, 33). The reason is probably that women by nature have a greater capacity for love.

Love Is Kind

One of the primary characteristics of love is kindness. Somehow, many of those having trouble in marriage have

112

forgotten to show kindness. They want to receive it, but they forget to give it. A couple who had been married two years came in to see me, fulfilling the promise that I require of all young couples before marriage that before they separate from each other they come and talk the matter over with me. They were ready to call it quits even though they sensed they had a little love left in their marriage. The problem was, they were very caustic, sarcastic, and cutting in their speech toward each other. When this was revealed in counseling, I gave them the assignment of memorizing the nine characteristics of love and, since kindness to each other was conspicuously absent, I asked them to give their conversation "the kindness check." That is, every time they said something to each other they were to ask themselves, "Was that kind?" If not, they were to apologize and seek God's grace to be kind. Obviously it was difficult for a time, but within two months this couple had reoriented themselves to the point that they could be kind to each other and the result was a renewing of their genuine affection for each other.

Love Shows Approval

Most psychologists agree that the basic needs of man are love and approval. The more we love someone, the more we naturally seek his approval. For that reason, if a person does not express his love by showing approval occasionally, he will have a dissatisfied mate.

A couple came to see me one time that were complete opposites physically. The man was six-feet-four and weighed at least 235 pounds—a real football type. The woman could not have weighed over 105 pounds and was probably about five feet tall. In the course of counseling, he said in an emotion packed voice, "Pastor, I haven't hit that woman in all the years we have been married," and as he said it he doubled up his gigantic fist. I looked at her, and saw tears running down her cheeks as she dejectedly said, "That's true, but many times I wish he had hit me instead of everlastingly clubbing me with disapproval!"

I honestly believe that disapproval is a more vicious way of inflicting punishment upon another human being than physical abuse. And the sad part is, the thing people disapprove of in their partner is usually blown up out of proportion, making the problem greater than it is. Many a man would have to admit that he has a good wife, and the thing that aggravates him comprises only ten to fifteen percent of the total person. His problem is that he has concentrated too much on the negative instead of thanking God for the positive. It is good to frequently ask yourself, "Do I express approval of my partner?" That approval should be expressed both publicly, to assure your friends that you love your partner, and privately. Many a man has been given a neater house by commending his wife for those areas that are neat rather than condemning her for those that are messy. Be sure of one thing, your partner needs your approval for his or her adjustment in life and marriage. Most people respond better to commendation than to condemnation.

Love Can Be Rekindled

"I just don't love my husband any more!" said a young woman whose husband was not a Chrisian. She was looking for the wrong way of escape—divorce. Not loving your partner does not necessarily testify to the unloveliness of the partner, but it does reveal your own lack of love. God will give you love for your partner if you seek it! As we have already seen, love is of God (I John 4:7). If you want to love your partner, you can! God has commanded you to love him, or her, and he will enable you to if you ask him. In fact, the first characteristic of the spirit-filled life is "love" (Galatians 5:22). If you find your love beginning to wane then go to your heavenly Father, the author of love, and he will give you a new love for your partner. It is yours for the asking! You may be inclined to ask, "But is it worth it?" or "What if my partner doesn't deserve it?" That has nothing to do with it. You should love your partner for the Lord's sake; but, because of the principle of reaping what you sow, loving will bring you love. If you go to God by faith for his supply of love to give to your partner, then God's divine law will bring love to you.

The young woman previously mentioned prayed with me for that kind of love, and God gave it. Just the other night after a service she said to me, "You just wouldn't believe the way God has returned my love for my husband! In fact, he has never been more loving and considerate in the eight years we have been married."

Women Respond To Love

I never cease to marvel at the endurance of a woman's love. Women have told me things about their husbands that could earn them the title, "the meanest man in town," yet these women end up by saying, "but I still love him." Men would never put up with some of the things that most women are forced to endure. It must be a carry over of a mother's love which we tend to think of as the greatest illustration of human love. Whatever the cause, I am convinced that a woman has a far greater capacity to love a man than a man has to love a woman. I have yet to see a woman who will not respond to love.

No man in his right mind would present himself as an authority on women. Most of us say they are complex creatures and they are. Like other men I do not claim to be an authority on feminine matters, but after counseling several hundred of the so-called "weaker sex" I have come to one basic conclusion. Most American men do not know how to make a woman happy. I have learned that it isn't money, diamonds, furs, houses, or other things that make a woman happy, but just plain love. Not love making, but the treatment that produces love making—kindness, thoughtfulness, understanding, acceptance or approval, and the recognition on the part of the husband that he is just not complete without her. Happy is the wife whose husband knows and tells her that if given the chance to marry all over again, he would choose the same bride. Whenever a man tells me, "My wife doesn't love me anymore," I immediately know that he is a man who has not loved his wife "as his own body." If he had, she would return his love—that's just the nature of women.

COMMUNICATION

Young lovers rarely have a communication problem! They seem to be able to talk about anything. Somehow, that ability often vanishes after they are married.

Lack of communication is almost always a problem for the couples who come to me for marriage counseling. If it is not lack of communication, it is wrong communication. Communicating under pressure of anger and shouting at the top of one's voice is the wrong approach. This is communication that could well be omitted in every marriage. Problems and differences in a marriage are not dangerous—not being able to communicate the differences, or problem areas, is dangerous. As long as two people can keep the lines of communication open and freely express their feelings, differences can be resolved.

The following statement by Ann Landers in her syndicated column illustrates the importance of communication. "The most important single ingredient in a marriage is the ability to communicate. If my mail is a fair reflection of what goes on with Mr. and Mrs. America behind closed doors (and I think it is), most marital problems stem from the inability of two people to talk to each other. How precious is the ability to communicate! . . . The mature man and woman recognize that there is unity in love, but at the same time there must be freedom for both individuals. Neither should be swallowed up by the other. Each must maintain his personality and his identity. A sound marriage should mean togetherness, but it also should mean respect for the rights and privileges of the other party. The couples who are secure in marriage can be honest about all kinds of feelings. . . The man and wife who can air their differences, get the hostility out of their system, then kiss and make up have an excellent chance of growing old together."

It has been amazing to me to find that many couples settle for a second-rate marriage relationship primarily because they have never learned to communicate. A few years ago a woman, who did not know I had already talked with her husband, came to me for counseling. Their problem seemed to be that the woman was not completely committed to the Lord. But her lack of commitment to Christ was not the real problem. A few weeks later she gave me a ride home after a meeting and spontaneously invited me in to talk to both of them. Her husband was surprised, but quickly responded; and suddenly I was acting as a referee between two friends. For twenty minutes she calmly mentioned some of her pet gripes and objections to her husband. None of them were unusual or severe but added together created a spirit of resentment in her. Some things went back to within six months after they were married. When she finished, he very calmly said to her, "Honey, why in the world didn't you tell me these things years ago?" (They had been married ten years.) Her answer was, "I was afraid to. I thought you would explode."

Knowing that every argument has two sides, I asked the husband if he would like to voice his objections to her as kindly as he could. For a similar period of time he then rehearsed her weaknesses and when he finished, she turned and said, "Why didn't you tell me this before?" He replied, "Because I thought you would get mad and go into a long period of silence." By learning to communicate, that couple soon learned to exchange their honest feelings without fear and the wife was able to fully commit herself to Christ.

Communication Killers

How does the wall of resistance to communication gradually build up between two people that love each other? Naturally, neither plans the erection of such a wall; it gradually grows from the time of their first breakdown in communication. Dr. Henry Brandt shared with a group of ministers the three weapons that people use to defend themselves. As you look at these three weapons you will find that by using them married people gradually build a wall of resistance so they are no longer able to communicate.

The first weapon is *explosion*. Whenever a person is told his shortcomings, rather than face them honestly, his natural reaction is to explode. This explosion is the result of inner anger and hostility that causes him to attempt self-protection. Dr. Brandt points out that no nakedness is comparable to psychological nakedness. When someone, particularly our partner, points out our deficiencies we tend to grasp for something to cover us; and if we happen to be sanguine or choleric in temperament we will tend to utilize anger and express it through explosion. What this does is teach our partner that "you can't come that close to my intimate weaknesses; if you do, I'll explode."

The second self-defense weapon that hinders communication is *tears*. This weapon is used mostly by women, though sometimes a melancholy or sanguine man will resort to it. Like the other weapons, it is a way of saying to your partner, "Don't tell me my shortcomings or I'll cry!" The first spat after marriage often leaves the bride in tears. This teaches the new husband that she has a breaking point and subconsciously he will thereafter tend to hold back his communication lest he make her cry. Thus, another brick is laid in the wall that stifles communication.

A parenthetical note is appropriate here on feminine tears. Husband, learn to distinguish between your wife's tears of emotion, stress, joy and self-pity. Women are far more intricate creatures than men, and often show their emotions through tears. Don't despise your wife's tears! Be patient and kind, for the emotional creature you married is just being a woman. In fact, I have found that the woman who is easily moved to tears has the greatest capacity to express her emotions in every area of life. Usually that type of wife is more responsive to tenderness and love-making than the dry-eyed girl. In fact, years ago I came to the conclusion that women who weep easily are seldom frigid, and tearless wives often have emotions like an iceberg. Since that time I have counseled more than one thousand women and have had no reason to change my conclusion. If your wife is emotionally expressive, thank God! Her tears testify to this emotional richness that make her a compassionate mother and loving wife. Be particularly thoughtful during her menstrual period, as she may be unusually emotional then. "Tender loving care" (T.L.C.) during that period is like laying up treasure in heaven—it pays off by and by.

The third weapon is *silence*. Silence is the weapon that many older Christians learn to use. It is not long before we realize that it isn't Christian to get mad and explode all over the neighborhood when our partner crosses us or points out our weaknesses. Then too, as children come along we are reluctant to weep in front of them; therefore, Christians resort to silence. Silence, however, is a very dangerous tool. It is dangerous in that it rapidly stifles communication and takes a heavy toll physically and spiritually upon a person. It takes tremendous power to be silent for a long period of time; anger can supply that power. Since anger is one of the leading causes of ulcers, high blood pressure and many other diseases you will find that silence is a very expensive tool to use on your partner.

Some years ago I counseled with a couple and one of their problems was that the man was very slow of speech and his wife was just the opposite. Whenever he would try to express himself, she couldn't wait but would give the rebuttal to his statement even before he had finished. In fact, her constant chatter often reminded me of a machine gun as she blasted away at him. He soon learned that he was no match for her in an argument. One day I met him at church and just casually asked, "How are things going?" "Wonderful," he said. "I finally found out how to handle that woman!"

When I asked him how he did it, he said, "Through silence. The one thing she can't stand is for me to be silent.

When she crosses me I will go for long periods without talking. In fact, I even went five days one time without speaking to her." My answer to him was, "That is going to be a very expensive tool because pent-up anger and bitterness produce ulcers." Little did I realize how prophetic my statement was, for in a matter of weeks I got the report that he had a bleeding ulcer.

How much better it would be if two people would learn to freely communicate their differences, and thereby avoid not only problems but also the side effects. Remember, all anger, bitterness, and wrath grieve the Holy Spirit (Ephesians 4:30-32). No man can walk in the Spirit and be mad at his wife (Galatians 5:16).

How To Communicate

The Bible teaches that we should "speak the truth in love..." (Ephesians 4:15). One should bear in mind, however, that the more truth you would speak, the more love you should use in conveying that truth. Truth is a sharp two-edged sword, so use it carefully. When you have an area in your marriage that needs communication, consider using the following steps in presenting your case.

• Pray for the wisdom of God and the filling of the Holy Spirit. When you seek God's wisdom you may find that your objection to your partner's behavior is not really valid. Or, you may sense the leading of the Spirit of God to go ahead and communicate your problem.

• Plan a time that is good for your partner. Usually you should not discuss anything of a serious or negative nature after 10:00 or 10:30 p.m. Life tends to look darker and problems loom greater at night. However, if your partner is not an early riser, the morning is not the best time either.

121

Many couples find that after supper is a good time for communication. Small children can often make this less than desirable, but each couple should find a time when they are in the best possible mood to look objectively at themselves.

- Speak the truth in love—in kind words say exactly what is on your heart. Make sure that your love is equal to your truth.

- Don't lose your temper. Wise couples determine early in their marriage that they will not raise their voices at each other. Under anger we often say more than we intend and usually this excess is cutting, cruel, and unnecessary. Anger on one person's part usually precipitates an angry response by the other. Kindly state your objection in love but state it only once, then trust the Holy Spirit to use your words in effecting a change.

- Allow for reaction time. Don't be surprised if your communication is met with an explosive reaction, particularly in the earlier stages of marriage. Remember, you have the advantage in that you know what you are going to say; you have prayed it over and have been able to prepare yourself— your partner is taken by surprise. Don't defend yourself, but let your partner think about what you have said. He may never admit that you are right but usually you will find that it will create a change in his behavior and after all, you are more interested in that than you are in verbal agreement.

- Commit the problem to God. Once you have told your partner, you have done about all you can do, humanly speaking, to change his behavior. From that point on you must trust God either to help your partner change his objectionable habit or to supply you with the necessary grace to live with it (II Corinthians 12:9).

122

Two Golden Expressions

There are two golden expressions that every married couple should communicate to their partner repeatedly throughout their marriage.

I'm sorry. Everyone makes mistakes. Romans 3:23 points out that "all have sinned, and come short of the glory of God." You will sin against your partner and your partner will sin against you many times in a normal marriage. If, however, you are willing to face your mistakes and apologize to your companion, you will find resistance dissolve and a spirit of forgiveness will prevail. If you are unwilling to acknowledge your mistakes, then you have a serious spiritual problem—pride.

One time I counseled with a couple and the wife tearfully said, "My husband has never apologized to me in the twenty-three years we have been married." Turning to him, I asked him if he had ever done anything wrong. He quickly replied, "Oh, of course, I am only human." I then asked, "Why have you never apologized?" His reply was, "I didn't think it was very manly for me to apologize; my father never apologized to my mother." Unfortunately, this man grew up under a father that made a very terrible decision never to apologize. Now this man was perpetuating that mistake and reaping the resultant misery. When you are wrong, face it objectively and honestly admit it—both to yourself and to your partner.

I love you is the second golden expression in a marriage. I have already pointed out that it is absolutely necessary for every human being to be loved. Your partner will never tire of hearing you tell him or her of your love. This expression of love seems to be more meaningful to women than men, but I am inclined to believe women are just more prone to admit the need for it, and that men need it also.

A man came in to see me the day after his wife of fifteen years had left him. He was a brilliant engineer with an I.Q. of 148 he said, and made "$15,000 a year." As he told me about the shipwreck of his marriage he acknowledged that he had not told his wife he loved her for ten years. When I asked him why, he said, "Why should I have to tell her? I have demonstrated it faithfully for fifteen years. She didn't like the house we lived in, so I bought her another house. She didn't like her car, so I bought her another car to run around in. She didn't like the carpeting, so I had it taken out and new carpeting put in. If I didn't love her would I have given her five children?"

The amazing thing about the whole affair was that his wife had run off with a sailor who made $275.00 a month and looked enough like her husband to be his twin brother. In exasperation he said to me, "What could that poor sailor possibly give to my wife that I haven't already given her?" My answer was, "Just one thing, love."

As brilliant a scientist as he was, this man was an ignoramus as a husband. Their problem could have been absolved if he had been willing to give of himself and let her know that he loved her and approved of her. He couldn't seem to understand that although saying "I love you" sounded childish to him, it was meaningful to her. Nor did he understand that if he had not been so selfish he would have been more than willing to express in words what she wanted to hear. The more your partner loves you the more he enjoys hearing you express your love. Say it meaningfully and say it often.

PRAYER

I have already discussed prayer under the subject Spiritual Adjustment so I will not enter into a lengthy dissertation here. However, keys to a happy marriage would not be complete if I did not include prayer. Prayer to their heavenly Father is the best means of communication between two people. Many a marriage has been completely transformed by initiating a practice of regular prayer. One method I heartily recommend is conversational prayer. I learned about this method from an article in *King's Business* about the prayer life of Dr. and Mrs. Ralph Byron. Dr. Byron is Chief Surgeon at the City of Hope Cancer Hospital in Los Angeles, California. My wife and I inaugurated this method with a slight modification and have found it to be a tremendous blessing. Here is how it works: each night one person leads the prayer time by praying for one subject at a time. The other partner then prays for the same subject. The first one then prays for the next burden of his heart and his partner again prays for the same thing. This procedure is continued until they have prayed for about five to ten things. The next night it is the other partner's turn to initiate prayer burdens and thus by praying specifically for the burden of the other person's heart it isn't long before they are both burdened for the same thing. My wife and I found that after a few weeks we couldn't always remember who had a burden first, but came to identify ourselves with each other's burdens. Another blessing we discovered was that in prayer we were reminded to share things that we had forgotten to share because of the busy activities of life. This sharing further broadens the common bond that exists between a husband and wife.

Having reached a stalemate with two of the couples I was counseling, I decided to ask them to try this method of prayer. One couple started that very night, and within a week called to say they didn't feel they needed to come in for counseling any more because the "Lord has solved our difficulties." The other couple refused to enter into this prayer relationship and though many months have passed it is quite apparent they are still living in an "armed truce."

Someone has said, "You can't quarrel with the woman you have prayed with every day." There is something humbling about getting down on your knees together; it is emotionally beneficial to both parties. Many a couple has acknowledged they rise from their knees more genuinely intertwined than before they prayed. Try it and see.

Who should initiate prayer? Ordinarily the husband, the head of the home; but if he doesn't, the wife can. The time spent in prayer together can very well be the most valuable time of your lives. Don't wait until the complexities of life drive you to your knees. If you wait until some difficulty arises to pray together, you will find that when you need God most you know him least. Learn to know him together in prayer now so that when life's pressure is on, you can go in prayer to one you have already learned to know as a close friend.

CHRIST

Things equal to the same thing are equal to each other is a well-known geometric principle. If two people are properly related in a personal way to Jesus Christ, they will most likely be properly related to each other. Jesus Christ wants to be LORD and SAVIOR of you as an individual. Then, he wants to be the LORD of your marriage. If he is, then the home you are building will abide in lasting peace and blessing. If he is not the spiritual head of your home, you will find that you will never experience all of the blessing that

God has for you in marriage. Jesus said, "Without Me ye can do nothing" (John 15:5).

If you have never received Jesus Christ, may I suggest that right now you bow your head and invite him into your life. He said, "Behold, I stand at the door, and knock: if any man hear my voice, and open the door, I will come in to him, and will sup with him, and he with me" (Revelation 3:20). If you desire him to come into your life, all you need do is ask him. Once inside, he then, by his Spirit, will direct you in all areas of life and will "supply all your need."

The test of all marital behavior in relationship to Christ should be, "Is it done with his approval?" The Scripture teaches, "And whatsoever ye do in word or deed, do all in the name of the Lord Jesus, giving thanks to God and the Father by him" (Colossians 3:17). Jesus Christ is interested in every area of your life: physical, emotional, financial, and spiritual. Living in accordance with his will as revealed in his Word, is the most important thing you can do to insure a happy marriage. You can then say:

> Christ is the head of this house,
>
> The unseen guest at every meal,
>
> The silent listener to every conversation.

Without a doubt, Christ is the greatest key to happiness in marriage.

If you ask God to help you utilize these six keys in your life and marriage, your home will become increasingly blessed and happy.

APPENDIX A/
THE SPIRIT-FILLED PERSON

The most important thing in the life of any Christian is to be filled with the Holy Spirit![1] The Lord Jesus said, "Without me ye can do nothing." Christ is in believers in the person of his Holy Spirit. Therefore, if we are filled with his Spirit, he works fruitfully through us. If we are not filled with the Holy Spirit, we are unproductive.

It is almost impossible to exaggerate how dependent we are on the Holy Spirit. We are dependent on him for convicting us of sin before and after our salvation, for giving us understanding of the Gospel, causing us to be born again, empowering us to witness, guiding us in our prayer life—in fact, for everything. It is no wonder that evil spirits have tried to counterfeit the work of the Holy Spirit and confuse his work.

There is probably no subject in the Bible upon which there is more confusion today than that of being filled with the Holy Spirit. Satan places two obstacles before men: (1) he tries to keep them from receiving Christ as Savior, and (2) if he fails in this, he then tries to keep men from understanding the importance and work of the Holy Spirit. Once a man is converted, Satan seems to have two different approaches. He tries to get men to associate the filling of the Holy Spirit with emotional excesses, or, the opposite swing of the pendulum, to ignore the Holy Spirit altogether.

[1]This appendix is a chapter from Tim LaHaye's previous book, SPIRIT-CONTROLLED TEMPERAMENT.

One of the false impressions gained from people and not from the Word of God is that there is some special "feeling" when one is filled with the Holy Spirit. Before we examine how to be filled with the Holy Spirit, let us find what the Bible teaches we can expect when we are filled with the Holy Spirit.

What To Expect When Filled With The Holy Spirit

1. The nine temperament traits of the Spirit-filled life as found in Galatians 5:22-23 are love, joy, peace, long-suffering (patience), gentleness, goodness, faith, meekness, temperance (self-control).

Any individual who is filled with the Holy Spirit is going to manifest these characteristics! He does not have to try to, or play a part, or act out a role; he will just be this way when the Spirit has control of his nature.

Many who claim to have had the "filling," or as some call it, "the anointing," know nothing of love, joy, peace, longsuffering, gentleness, goodness, meekness, faith, or self-control. These are, however, the hallmark of the person filled with the Holy Spirit!

2. A joyful, thanks-giving heart and a submissive spirit (Ephesians 5:18-21).

When the Holy Spirit fills the life of a believer, the Bible tells us he will cause him to have a singing, thanksgiving heart and a submissive spirit.

> And be not drunk with wine, wherein is excess; but be filled with the Spirit;
> Speaking to yourselves in psalms and hymns and spiritual songs, singing and making melody in your heart to the Lord;
> Giving thanks always for all things unto God and

the Father in the name of our Lord Jesus Christ;
Submitting yourselves one to another in the fear of
God.

A singing, thanks-giving heart and a submissive spirit,
independent of circumstances, are so unnatural that they can
only be ours through the filling of the Holy Spirit. The
Spirit of God is able to change the gloomy or griping heart
into a song-filled, thankful heart. He is also able to solve
man's natural rebellion problem by increasing his faith to the
point that he really believes the best way to live is in submission to the will of God.

The same three results of the Spirit-filled life are also
the results of the Word-filled life, as found in Colossians
3:16-18.

Let the word of Christ dwell in you richly in all
wisdom; teaching and admonishing one another in
psalms and hymns and spiritual songs, singing with
grace in your hearts to the Lord.
And whatsoever ye do in word or deed, do all in the
name of the Lord Jesus, giving thanks to God and
the Father by him.
Wives, submit yourselves unto your own husbands,
as it is fit in the Lord.

It is no accident that we find the results of the Spirit-
filled life (Ephesians 5:18-21) and those of the Word-filled
life to be one and the same. The Lord Jesus said that the
Holy Spirit is "the Spirit of Truth," and he also said of the
Word of God, "Thy Word is Truth." It is easily understood
why the Word-filled life causes the same results as the Spirit-
filled life, for the Holy Spirit is the author of the Word of
God. This highlights the error of those who try to receive
the Holy Spirit through a once-for-all experience rather than

an intimate relationship with God which Jesus described as "abiding in Me." This relationship is possible in the Christian's life as God communes with him and fills his life through the "Word of Truth" and as he communes with God in prayer guided by the "Spirit of Truth." The conclusion that we can clearly draw here is that the Christian who is Spirit-filled will be Word-filled, and the Word-filled Christian who obeys the Spirit will be Spirit-filled.

3. The Holy Spirit gives us power to witness (Acts 1:8):

> But ye shall receive power, after that the Holy Ghost is come upon you: and ye shall be witnesses unto Me both in Jerusalem, and in all Judaea, and in Samaria, and unto the uttermost part of the earth.

The Lord Jesus told his disciples that "It is expedient (necessary) for you that I go away: for if I go not away, the Comforter (Holy Spirit) will not come unto you" (John 16:7). That explains why the last thing Jesus did before he ascended into heaven was to tell his disciples, "But ye shall receive power, after that the Holy Spirit is come upon you: and ye shall be witnesses unto me..."

Even though the disciples had spent three years with Jesus personally, had heard his messages several times, and were the best trained witnesses he had, he still instructed them "not to depart from Jerusalem, but wait for the promise of the Father" (Acts 1:4). All of their training obviously was incapable of producing fruit of itself without the power of the Holy Spirit. It is well known that when the Holy Spirit came on the day of Pentecost, they witnessed in His power, and three thousand persons were saved.

We too can expect to have power to witness when filled with the Holy Spirit. Would to God that there was as much desire on the part of God's people to be empowered to witness in the Spirit as there is to have some ecstatic or emotional experience with the Holy Spirit.

The power to witness in the Holy Spirit is not always discernable, but must be accepted by faith. When we have met the conditions for the filling of the Holy Spirit, we should be careful to believe we have witnessed in the power of the Spirit whether or not we see the results. Because the Holy Spirit demonstrated his presence on the day of Pentecost so dramatically and because occasionally we see the evidence of the Holy Spirit in our lives, we come to think that it should always be obvious, but that is not true. It is possible to witness in the power of the Holy Spirit and still not see an individual come to a saving knowledge of Christ. For in the sovereign plan of God he has chosen never to violate the right of man's free choice. Therefore, a man can be witnessed to in the power of the Holy Spirit and still reject the Savior. The witness may then go away with the erroneous idea of having been powerless merely because he was unsuccessful. We cannot always equate success in witnessing with the power to witness!

Recently it was my privilege to witness to an 80-year-old man. Because of his age and a particular problem, I made a special effort to meet the conditions of being filled with the Holy Spirit before I went to his home. He paid very close attention as I presented the Gospel by using the "four spiritual laws." When I finished and asked if he would like to receive Christ right then, he said, "No, I'm not ready yet." I went away amazed that a man 80 years of age could say he was "not ready yet" and concluded that I did not witness in the power of the Holy Spirit.

A short time later I went back to see the man and found that he had passed his 81st birthday. Once again I started to present the Gospel to him, but he informed me that he had received Christ. He had restudied the four spiritual laws which I had written out on a sheet of paper, and alone in his room he got down on his knees and invited Christ Jesus into his life as Savior and Lord. Afterward, I wondered how many other times in my life, because I had not seen an immediate response to the Gospel, I had wrongly concluded that the Spirit had not filled me with his power to witness.

To be sure, a Christian life, when filled with the Holy Spirit, will produce fruit. For if you examine what Jesus referred to as "abide in me" (John 15) and what the Bible teaches in relationship to being "filled with the Spirit," you will find they are one and the same experience. Jesus said, "He that abideth in me, and I in him, the same bringeth forth much fruit..." Therefore, we can conclude that the abiding life or the Spirit-filled life will produce fruit. But it is wrong to require every witnessing opportunity to demonstrate whether or not we are empowered by the Spirit to witness. Instead, we must meet the conditions for the filling of the Holy Spirit and then believe, not by results or sight or feeling, but by faith, that we are filled.

4. The Holy Spirit will glorify Jesus Christ (John 16:13-14):
   Howbeit when He, the Spirit of truth, is come, He
   will guide you into all truth; for He shall not speak
   of Himself; but whatsoever He shall hear, that shall
   He speak: and He will shew you things to come.
   He shall glorify Me: for He shall receive of Mine,
   and shall shew it unto you.

A fundamental principle should always be kept in mind regarding the work of the Holy Spirit: he does not glorify himself, but the Lord Jesus Christ. Any time anyone but the Lord Jesus receives the glory, you can be sure that what is done is not done in the power of or under the direction of the Holy Spirit, for his express work is to glorify Jesus. This test should always be given to any work that claims to be the work of God's Holy Spirit.

The late F. B. Meyer told the story of a woman missionary who came to him at a Bible conference after he had spoken on the subject of how to be filled with the Holy Spirit. She confessed that she was never consciously filled with the Holy Spirit and was going to go up to the prayer chapel and spend the day in soul-searching to see if she could receive his filling.

Late that evening she came back just as Meyer was leaving the auditorium. He asked, "How was it, sister?" and she said, "I'm not quite sure." He then asked what she did, and she explained her day's activities of reading the Word, praying, confessing her sins and asking for the filling of the Holy Spirit. She then stated, "I do not feel filled with the Holy Spirit." Meyer asked her, "Tell me, sister, how is it between you and the Lord Jesus?" Her face lit up and with a smile she said, "Oh, Dr. Meyer, I have never had a more blessed time of fellowship with the Lord Jesus in all of my life." To which he replied, "Sister, that is the Holy Spirit!" The Holy Spirit will always make the believer more conscious of the Lord Jesus than himself.

Now, in review, let us summarize what we can expect when filled with the Holy Spirit. Very simply, it is the nine temperament characteristics of the Spirit, a singing, thanksgiving heart that gives us a submissive attitude, and the power to witness. These characteristics will glorify the Lord Jesus Christ. What about "feeling" or "ecstatic experiences"? The Bible does not tell us to expect these things when we are filled with the Holy Spirit; therefore, we should not expect that which the Bible does not promise.

135

How To Be Filled With The Holy Spirit

The filling of the Holy Spirit is not optional equipment in the Christian life, but a command of God! Ephesians 5:18 tells us, "And be not drunk with wine, wherein is excess, but be filled with the Spirit." This statement is in the imperative mood; thus we should accept it as a command.

God never makes it impossible for us to keep his commandments. So, obviously, if he commands us to be filled with the Holy Spirit, and he does, then it must be possible for us to be filled with his Spirit. I would like to give five simple steps for being filled with the Holy Spirit:

1. Self-examination (Acts 20:28 and I Corinthians 11:28):

The Christian interested in the filling of the Holy Spirit must regularly "take heed" to "examine himself." He should examine himself, not to see if he measures up to the standards of other people or the traditions and requirements of his church, but to the previously mentioned results of being filled with the Holy Spirit. If he does not find he is glorifying Jesus, if he does not have power to witness, or if he lacks a joyful, submissive spirit or the nine temperament traits of the Holy Spirit, then his self-examination will reveal those areas in which he is deficient and will uncover the sin that causes them.

2. Confession of all known sin (I John 1:9):

If we confess our sins, He is faithful and just to forgive us our sins, and to cleanse us from all unrighteousness.

The Bible does not put an evaluation on one sin or another, but seems to judge all sin alike. After examining ourselves in the light of the Word of God, we should confess all sin brought to mind by the Holy Spirit, including those characteristics of the Spirit-filled life that we lack. Until we start calling our lack of compassion, our lack of self-control, our lack of humility, our anger instead of gentleness, our bitterness instead of kindness, and our unbelief instead of faith, as sin, we will never have the filling of the Holy Spirit. However, the moment we recognize these deficiencies as sin and confess them to God, he will "cleanse us from all un-righteousness." Until we have done this we cannot have the filling of the Holy Spirit, for he fills only clean vessels (II Timothy 2:21).

3. Submit yourself completely to God (Romans 6:11-13):

Likewise reckon ye also yourselves to be dead indeed unto sin, but alive unto God through Jesus Christ our Lord.

Let not sin therefore reign in your mortal body, that ye should obey it in the lusts thereof.

Neither yield ye your members as instruments of unrighteousness unto sin: but yield yourselves unto God, as those that are alive from the dead, and your members as instruments of righteousness unto God.

To be filled with the Holy Spirit, one must make himself completely available to God to do anything the Holy Spirit directs him to do. If there is anything in your life that you are unwilling to do or to be, then you are resisting God, and this always limits God's Spirit! Do not make the mistake of being afraid to give yourself to God! Romans 8:32 tells us, "He that spared not His own Son, but delivered Him up for us all, how shall He not with Him also freely give us all things?" It is clear from this verse that if God loved us so much as to give his Son to die for us, certainly he is inter-ested in nothing but our good; therefore, we can trust him with our lives. You will never find a miserable Christian in the center of the will of God, for he will always accompany his directions with an appetite and desire to do his will.

Resisting the Lord through rebellion obviously stifles the

filling of the Spirit. Israel limited the Lord, not only through unbelief, but, as Psalm 78:8 tells us, by becoming a "stubborn and rebellious generation; a generation that set not their heart aright and whose spirit was not steadfast with God." All resistance to the will of God will keep us from being filled with the Holy Spirit. To be filled with his Spirit, we must yield ourselves to his Spirit just as a man yields himself to wine for its filling.

Ephesians 5:18 says, "Be not drunk with wine...but be filled with the Spirit." When a man is drunk, he is dominated by alcohol; he lives and acts, and is dominated by its influence. So with the filling of the Holy Spirit, man's actions must be dominated by and dictated by the Holy Spirit. For consecrated Christians this is often the most difficult thing to do, for we can always find some worthy purpose for our lives, not realizing that we are often filled with ourselves rather than with the Holy Spirit, as we seek to serve the Lord.

This summer, while speaking at a high school and college camp, we had a thrilling testimony from a ministerial student who said that for the first time he realized what it meant to be filled with the Holy Spirit. As far as he knew, he had not been guilty of the usual sins of the carnal Christian. Actually, he had only one area of resistance in his life. He loved to preach, and the possibilities of being a pastor or evangelist appealed to him very much, but he did not want the Lord to make a missionary out of him. During that week the Holy Spirit spoke to the lad about that very vocation, and when he submitted everything to the Lord and said, "Yes, I'll go to the ends of the earth," for the first time he experienced the true filling of the Holy Spirit. He then went on to say, "I don't believe the Lord wants me to be a missionary after all; he just wanted me to be willing to be a missionary."

When you give your life to God, do not attach any strings or conditions to it. He is such a God of love that you can safely give yourself without reservation, knowing that his plan and use of your life is far better than yours. And, remember, the attitude of yieldedness is absolutely necessary for the filling of God's Spirit. Your will is the will of the flesh, and the Bible says that "the flesh profiteth nothing."

Yieldedness is sometimes difficult to determine when once we have solved the five big questions of life: (1) Where shall I attend college? (2) What vocation shall I pursue? (3) Whom shall I marry? (4) Where shall I live? (5) Where shall I attend church? A Spirit-filled Christian will be sensitive to the Spirit's leading in small decisions as well as the big ones. But it has been my observation that many Christians who have made the right decisions on life's five big questions are still not filled with the Spirit.

Someone has suggested that being yielded to the Spirit is being available to the Spirit. Peter and John in Acts 3 make a good example of that. They were on their way to the temple to pray when they saw the lame man begging alms. Because they were sensitive to the Holy Spirit, they healed him "in the name of Jesus Christ of Nazareth." The man began leaping about and praising God until a crowd gathered. Peter, still sensitive to the Holy Spirit, began preaching; "many of them which heard the Word believed; and the number of the men was about five thousand" (Acts 4:4).

Many times I fear we are so engrossed in some good Christian activity that we are not "available" when the Spirit leads. In my own life, I have found that when someone asks me to do some good thing and I give a negative response, it is the flesh rather than the Spirit. Many a Christian has said "no" to the Holy Spirit when he offered an opportunity to teach Sunday school. It may have been the Sunday school superintendent that asked, but he too had been seeking the leading of the Holy Spirit. Many a Christian says, "Lord, here am I, use me!" but when asked to go calling or witnessing is too busy painting, bowling, or pursuing some other activity that interferes. What is the problem? He just isn't available. When a Christian yields himself unto God, "as those that are alive from the dead," he takes time to do what the Spirit directs him to do.

4. Ask to be filled with the Holy Spirit (Luke 11:13):

> If ye, then, being evil, know how to give good gifts unto your children: how much more shall your heavenly Father give the Holy Spirit to them that ask him?"

When a Christian has examined himself, confessed all known sin and yielded himself without reservation to God, he is then ready to do the one thing he must do to receive the Spirit of God. Very simply, it is to ask to be filled with the Spirit. Any suggestion to present-day believers of waiting or tarrying or laboring or suffering is man's suggestion. Only the disciples were told to wait, and that was because the day of Pentecost had not yet come. Since that day, God's children have only to ask for his filling to experience it.

The Lord Jesus compares this to our treatment of our earthly children. Certainly a good father would not make his children beg for something he commanded them to have. How much less does God make us beg to be filled with the Holy Spirit which he has commanded. It is just as simple as that! But don't forget Step 5.

5. Believe you are filled with the Holy Spirit! And thank him for his filling.

> And he that doubteth is damned if he eat, because

he eateth not of faith: for whatsoever is not of faith
is sin (Romans 14:23).

In everything give thanks: for this is the will of God
in Christ Jesus concerning you (I Thessalonians
5:18).

For many Christians the battle is won or lost right here.
After examining themselves, confessing all known sin, yield-
ing themselves to God and asking for his filling, they are
faced with a decision: to believe they are filled, or to go
away in unbelief, in which case they have sinned, for "whatsoever is not of faith is sin."

The same Christian, who when doing personal work tells
the new convert to "take God at his Word concerning salvation," finds it difficult to heed his own advice concerning
the filling of the Holy Spirit. He will tell a new babe in
Christ, who lacks assurance of salvation, that he can know
that Christ is in his life because he promised to come in if
he were invited, and "God always keeps his Word." Oh,
that the same sincere personal worker would believe God
when he says: "How much more shall your heavenly Father
give the Holy Spirit to them that ask Him?" If you have
fulfilled the first four steps, then thank God for his filling by
faith. Don't wait for feelings, don't wait for any physical
signs, but fasten your faith to the Word of God that is independent of feeling. Feelings of assurance of the Spirit's filling
often follow our taking God at his Word and believing he
has filled us, but they neither cause the filling nor determine
whether or not we are filled. Believing we are filled with the
Spirit is merely taking God at his Word, and that is the only
absolute this world has (Matthew 24:35).

APPENDIX B/
FROM MY COUNSELING FILE

One of the greatest rewards for a minister is to see the power of Jesus Christ transform a depressingly miserable marriage into a happy one. A pastor sees this transformation more graphically in the counseling room than anywhere else. Every minister has his own philosophy of counseling and no one method is fool-proof. The stories that follow are true, although the names and revealing details have been modified to avoid betraying confidences. I want to share some of my principles for counseling and give a few case histories of successes and failures because I am convinced that a true story involving human beings in some way parallels the situations and happenings of others. Also these episodes will help illustrate the principles discussed in this book.

Pastoral counseling, to me, is a thrilling opportunity to assist people in the application of the principles of the Bible. Some people can accept the principles as preached in the church and make their own application. Others, because of background, temperament, and other factors need personal help in making these applications. When a person goes to see a medical doctor or a dentist he is basically seeking two things: diagnosis for the cause of his problem and a prescribed cure. I look upon people coming to a counselor much in the same manner. They want him to diagnose their problem and think he can do it more objectively because of his training and experience, and because he is not emotionally involved. When people come to a minister for counseling they usually expect him to give a remedy based on the Word of God. The secret of this therapy is really up to the patient. If he takes his medicine—or in the counseling situation if he accepts the principles of God, thus introducing the power of God into his life and marriage—then he can expect a cure. For that reason all counseling is not successful. Sometimes people refuse to accept the principles of God and incorporate them into their lives. Sometimes people agree that the principles are right but they are so stubbornly self-willed that they refuse to exchange their habits and way of life for God's ways. A doctor cannot do much for an obese patient who refuses to change his eating habits. Neither can a counselor do much for a selfish, domineering, fearful, or profligate person unless he is willing to face his shortcomings in the light of God's Word and then ask God for the power to change his habits and way of life.

Twenty-five-year Procrastination

After church one night a middle-aged man asked to see me. "I need God," he said. Later he told me that his father, a minister, had many times begged him to receive Christ, but he refused. Now after twenty-five years of marriage he realized he had been selfish, caustic, and cruel to his wife—and had destroyed his marriage. His wife had just told him she no longer loved him and was getting a divorce, so he felt he should come back to God. He knew the Gospel well. He received Christ by confessing his sin and inviting Jesus Christ into his life as Lord and Savior. I gave him some Scripture verses which assured him of his salvation and a few suggestions on how to read the Bible and pray. As he was leaving he asked, "Would you counsel with my wife?" "Naturally," I said.

144

When his wife walked into my study a few days later I was not quite prepared for her. A sharp looking owner-manager of a beauty shop she was every inch a dynamic human being. "I've had it," she said. "He has cursed me, hit me, belittled me, criticized me, scolded me and verbally harassed me until I have nothing but hatred in my heart for him. The sooner he gets out of my life the better off I will be." She had been planning and saving for years so that when her daughter finished high school, she would be financially independent. She had reached her goal of being "free to come and go as I please." She refused to talk of spiritual things because, she said, "If I accept Christ I will have to stay with him the rest of my life, and I'd roast in hell first. I never should have married him in the first place!"

I realized that this woman of choleric temperament had been miserable for many years. She doesn't know it, but worse days are ahead if she persists in her angry hostile self-will. Her melancholy husband had been a disappointment the first week of their marriage. Although he loved her, he continually found fault with her because she didn't meet his perfectionist standards. She was incensed at his criticism because he was so moody and indecisive that it took him forever to accomplish anything. Because she was the faster talker, she would lash him with words until he would become frustrated and strike her.

He comes to church regularly now and is growing spiritually by leaps and bounds. But everytime I see him I can't help thinking, "If only he had received Christ as a young man he would have been less selfish and critical and foregone all this heartache. Instead, he would have been more loving and kind to his wife and his home would not have been destroyed." So many couples are not aware that angry cruel words, like deep physical wounds, leave lasting scars.

The last chapter of this story has not yet been written. As I told the wife when she left after the last interview, "The Lord will be around to help you pick up the pieces of your life if you will just turn to him." Perhaps she will yet repent of her self-will and give God a chance to change her as he is changing her husband. How exciting it would be if they could live the next twenty-five years in marital happiness.

All such counseling doesn't end in permanent divorce. Three years ago I counseled a choleric woman and a melancholy man who were almost identical to the couple just mentioned, except they had been married only ten years. After a fling at being a cocktail waitress and doing whatever she wanted with her life she has finally faced the fact that at thirty-four years of age she was a very miserable woman. Her melancholy husband has grown so much spiritually that she could not help but see the change in him. When he came to visit the children she observed a new gentleness and thoughtfulness that was unknown before.

Now he is more patient, understanding, and considerate. In fact, he has a new air of confidence that makes it easier for him to make decisions and be flexible under pressure. She finally realized that Jesus Christ had so corrected her husband's weaknesses that he was superior to any of the other men she knew, so she asked for a reconciliation. Only Jesus Christ could give a man—particularly one with a melancholy temperament—the grace to forgive and forget those three years of sin.

Spiritual Lethargy

Another wife of choleric temperament came to see me one day and tearfully told how she and her husband were slowly drifting apart. She loved her husband, and felt he loved her, but said, "Another six months like this and we will hate each other." Her talented, but easy-going, husband was in business with his father. She and his father clashed over the way he was operating the business. She said to me, "If he keeps it up the way he is going we will soon be bankrupt." It seems a Christmas party at the in-laws had erupted into an explosion that almost equaled the blasts at the atomic testing grounds.

All of the folks involved were professing Christians. As we talked, she admitted her own spiritual lethargy and the awful anger and hostility that she permitted to run rampant in her life. From her point of view she had human justification to be angry. And, as she let things "fester and stew" in her mind, calm communication was impossible; instead she built up to such a point that she would explode with angry, sarcastic words that caused others unnecessary pain. She really didn't mean them and would like to have taken them back. We read and talked about Ephesians 4:30-32. She finally realized that all anger and wrath are sin. With that realization she took the first big step. She then understood that her job was to follow Christ's example and heed his instructions on being wife and mother—and not try to run her husband's business.

"But isn't there something I can do about the unchristian principles my father-in-law is bringing into our firm? I'm sure if he keeps this up he will destroy it! Do I have to sit back and do nothing?" were her honest questions. "Yes," I replied, "there are several things you can do. Get right with God yourself, concentrate on walking with him, and commit the business to him. When the Holy Spirit leads you, you might 'speak the truth in love' to your husband. But not in anger! Remember, he is caught in the crossfire of emotional loyalties between his parents and his wife. Your marriage is far more important than the business. It's your job to be a good wife, it's God's job to take care of the business. Concentrate on being a loving, gracious wife— and let God handle the business." I then shared with her how the Holy Spirit could overcome her weakness, and she went home.

Before long her husband began to realize that his wife had changed. As she relaxed and quit pressing him he lost his resentment toward her and the spark came back into their marriage. When he didn't hear her voice nagging him he could hear God speak to him about his spiritual indifference. As he grew spiritually he became alarmed about his father's business procedure and insisted on a change of policy. The business is now thriving, but more important is the change in this couple's relationship with each other and with God. Recently they sent one of their neighbors whom they had led to Christ to see me. When I asked what caused her to accept the Savior, she replied: "It's their home life, I never saw anything like it. These people have a love for each other that I have never seen before."

Fears Overcome

The power of Jesus Christ to cure fear is graphically illustrated in the wife of a neurologist in our city. Although Roman Catholic, she came to see me at the recommendation of some neighbors who are very faithful Christian witnesses. Her lifelong fears had developed into a phobia after her father committed suicide, and were gradually getting worse. She had experienced long periods of depression, become panicky of being alone, felt a strange muscular restriction when downtown surrounded by strange people and as she said, "I became phobic in elevators." Her fears caused her husband to draw away from her. Finally their marital situation came to a crisis when her doctor husband lost patience with her and angrily told her, "I have to deal with women like you all day. I don't want to come home to one every night."

Though terribly insecure she loved her husband dearly. Only God knows if she would have really kept her threats of self-destruction if he had left her. But she is so transformed today it is very doubtful that he wants to. During her first interview with me she invited Jesus Christ into her life. In subsequent interviews I pointed out some of the causes of her fears and prescribed God's method of cure.

At first it was hard for her to face the fact that her depression was caused by her thinking pattern of self-pity. When she told her story it wasn't hard to see that as a child she resented her father's drinking and developed the habit of feeling sorry for herself because of the unhappy life she and her mother lived. I showed her that if she faced her self-pity as a sin, confessed it (I John 1:9) and asked God to take away the habit of feeling sorry for herself (I John 5:14-15) that he would. Then I suggested she "forget those things that are behind and press on..." It took time, but she gradually learned how to give thanks (I Thessalonians 5:18) instead of complain. Depression soon began to lose its tyranical hold upon her. There are times when she forgets and reverts back to her old self-pity and is depressed, but it happens less frequently, and it is not nearly as severe as it was. If she continues growing in the Lord the cure will be permanent.

The fear problem was more complex. Part of it was caused by guilt feelings for the way she felt about her father before his death. This seemed to dissolve as she realized the

149

extent of her forgiveness as revealed in the Bible. Another part was gradually removed by doing a Bible study on fear and peace. As she realized that she had a constant companion who "sticketh closer than a friend or brother," that Jesus said, "I will never leave thee or forsake thee," and "Lo, I am with thee always," her life-long feeling of insecurity was being replaced by faith. She was fortunate in having a Christian friend who took her regularly to a women's Bible class. The Bible study and Christian friendship have been excellent therapy. Another part of her fear was helped by facing the fact that she was a very selfish woman. Basically, fear is caused by selfishness. As soon as the Holy Spirit came into her life he began to make her interested in other people. The more she lost herself in others, the less fearful she became.

It didn't take long for her analytically minded and medically trained husband to recognize that she had changed. He isn't ready to admit that a personal relationship with Jesus Christ has made the change in his wife, but he does concede that something has transformed her.

The power of Christ to overcome fear is not limited to a particular age. One day a woman two years short of retirement came in to say that she had received Christ in one of our women's Bible classes but guessed "that it didn't work." She had tried several religious and psychological approaches in order to overcome her fears, but none of them had helped her. Her fears kept her from sleeping and insomnia made her nervous and irritable. She had high blood pressure and worried constantly. She said, "The only thing that seems to help me is when I come over here late at night and sit on the front steps of the church and pray."

Her father, whom she loved and admired had been a liberal minister. He had taught that the Bible is a "good book, full of myths and legends, and should be taken symbolically." Consequently she couldn't understand and benefit from the Word of God because she invariably doubted everything she read. After several weekly interviews in which I gave her a spiritual prescription—reading at least ten minutes a day in the Bible and memorizing one verse of scripture —her life was changed. Then one day she said, "It's no longer necessary for you to see me, God has transformed my life." Everyone who knows her can see the change.

Misplaced Blame

A young businessman came in one day acknowledging his faults and weaknesses. Then he brought up his real problem: his wife was frigid. "It wasn't always this way," he said. "We met at a Christian group in college, and since we were too spiritual to go to shows and dance we could find little else to do on our dates but park and neck! It wasn't long before we began petting and that soon led to intercourse." They decided that rather than disgrace themselves and their families by an unwanted pregnancy they would get married. They avoided a premature family that way, but neither of them finished college. They gave up all thoughts of Christian service and his educational deficiency has seriously limited his vocational advancement. He concluded by saying that he tried to be thoughtful and kind, but that she was rapidly losing interest in any physical contact. Knowing there are always two sides to every marital problem I asked him to have his wife come see me.

When his wife of eleven years came in and tearfully cried, "I hate sex!", I knew she had some deep-rooted problems. Before discussing the physical maladjustment I asked a few questions about their children and marriage in general.

I recognized that she was a bundle of nerves bordering on neurosis because of her intense hostility and bitterness. She was completely frustrated. Every dream in life was smashed. She "wanted to be a virgin when I married, and just because he couldn't control his passion I lost that before we were married. I wanted to be a music teacher and wanted my husband to be a professional man, now neither of us qualify for anything! He is never home, he has to work two jobs to pay the bills, he never does anything around the house and we don't have a decent car, house or furniture. Nothing I dreamed of has worked out and it is all his fault!" Usually such an emotionally expressive woman has learned, after eleven years of marriage, to enjoy sex thoroughly, particularly when her husband is kind, clean and considerate.

It took some convincing to make Suzanne realize that although her husband had his faults and weaknesses, *her* attitude was the *real* problem. She felt excessive guilt for violating her courtship standards but instead of blaming herself, she blamed him. Instead of admitting that she could have said "no" while still assuring him of her love and waiting until they finished college to get married, she gave in because she wanted to. When she finally admitted her sin she was able to confess it and experienced a tremendous sense of relief. Through an examination of Ephesians 4:30-32 she saw her own hostility and "enmity of heart" as a sin that grieved the Holy Spirit. Gradually she learned to face anger as a sin and God began putting a new love into her heart for her husband. She began to relax and again became the emotionally-responsive wife that she had been on their honeymoon.

As they began praying together God has guided them in a long-range educational program that has given them new goals and objectives. The home that once was cold and hateful is now a haven. In fact, her husband admits that he used to seek any excuse to avoid spending time at home; now he tends to guard his opportunities to be with his wife and children because of the joy he experiences in being with them. Watching them as a pastor I have had my own satisfaction. Not only do they attend services more frequently, they no longer find some pretext to sit separately, but are always together.

Spirituality And Sex

It may strike some Christians as strange to hear a minister say that two Spirit-filled partners can experience more physical and emotional pleasure from the act of marriage than the average couple, but I definitely believe it. It is a well-known fact that relaxation and unselfishness are primary keys to sexual harmony. What power on earth can relax people and motivate them to goodness, kindness and self-control like the Holy Spirit? I have the impression that many Christians subconsciously think that when a couple experiences the filling of the Holy Spirit one of the first things they will do is rush out and buy a set of twin beds. This attitude implies that God put an evil drive in man. The truth of the matter is, the urge for the act of marriage is a gift of God for a couple's supreme emotional and physical pleasure. The more spiritually sensitive an ordinary Christian couple become, the more they may desire each other physically. When the Holy Spirit fills a life he puts a new love for other people in that heart. He makes a person more patient and kind. It naturally follows that a Spirit-filled husband is going to be more loving and affectionate to his wife, "the little things" that used to create hostility and resentment are gone; consequently, his wife has less emotional resistance to his sexual advances and is more likely to respond to his mood. In fact, a Spirit-filled woman will be less inhibited in the intimacies of marriage. Inhibitions tend to stifle sexual pleasure, particularly for a woman. Consequently, a Spirit-filled woman will gradually relax and more easily attain fulfillment in the experience.

As I look back on my counseling experience I remember only one Spirit-filled couple that came to me sexually maladjusted. They were a young couple who didn't know what they were doing. After we talked and they read two of the books listed at the end of Chapter 4 they solved their sexual problems.

Spiritually sensitive people are directed by the Holy Spirit to find the solutions to their problems. The spiritual characteristic of meekness overcomes the natural characteristic of pride that often keeps couples from admitting they have a problem. When they acknowledge the problem and seek God's help, he directs them to the right answer. Be sure you carefully read Appendix A on "How to be Filled with the Holy Spirit." It will enrich all areas of your marriage.

Hate Changes To Love

A few months ago I saw what is probably the best illustration of the power of Jesus Christ to change two people that I have ever seen. A young couple had been visiting our church off and on for about three months. One night they called and said they had to see me right away. I don't think I have ever been more conscious of blatant hatred between two people. There are three chairs in my study and when I said, "Won't you be seated," they wouldn't even sit next to each other, but purposely left the third seat vacant between them. It didn't take long for them to tell their story.

He very bluntly said, "She is a frigid woman! She won't let me touch her anymore." She said, "My father was an alcoholic. When we got married seven years ago he promised me he wouldn't drink if I married him. Now he drinks every night on the way home from work and on Friday nights he comes home drunk. I can't stand to have him touch me when he's been drinking." He fiercely snapped, "You were that way before I started drinking!" As we talked, it became apparent that they had two basic problems. They had other minor irritants, but basically they were sexually frustrated because of selfishness, ignorance, and lack of meaningful communication, and second, neither of them knew Jesus Christ as Savior. I didn't know which problem to tackle first, but remembered the sound advice of my high school football coach: "Never take on two men at the same time, always concentrate on one or the other." But which one, was the question. So I prayed, "Which problem do I take on first, Lord?" and it seemed I should talk with them about their sex life first.

They were married quite young and got along very well at first. But as the novelty of marriage wore off their different backgrounds came more to the surface. She was reared by very refined, religious people and liked etiquette, neatness, and a quiet household. She said, "I have never heard my parents raise their voices at each other, nor have I ever heard my father swear." The young man had been reared in a rough section of the city. Although he had not been loose in his morals prior to marriage, he had received his sex education in the alley and the Army barracks. Somehow she had never been able to tell him that his back alley words describing the intimacies of the marriage act "just turned her off!" Even though she was aroused, all he had to do was innocently say what she considered ugly words and her emotional fire went out. From then on she experienced intercourse as torture instead of pleasure and increasingly resisted him. The more she resisted him the more determined he became. Finally, after being rejected many times, he resorted to drinking just to get back at her.

His maturity was evident by his wholesome reaction as soon as he realized the effect his language had on her sensitive nature. He got up out of his chair, took the one closer to her and said, "Honey, I never dreamed that it was the things I said that offended you. I'm really sorry." She said, "I can't help it, but that's the way I feel." When she burst into tears he took her hand and earnestly said, "In front of Pastor I want to promise you that you will never hear me say those words again" (and interestingly enough she says that to date he has kept his word).

How To Become A Christian

That interchange cleared the air considerably, but I knew that good resolutions were not enough. They needed an external source of power to help them keep their vows. So I asked, "Have you folks ever heard of the Four Spiritual Laws?" Finding they had not I got out the little Four Laws booklet[1] I carry in my pocket and said, "Just as God has physical laws that govern his physical universe, so he has spiritual laws that govern his relationship to man." These are the laws I showed them.

1 *God Loves You, And Has A Wonderful Plan For Your*

[1]The diagrams and Four Spiritual Laws are copyrighted material and are used by permission of Campus Crusade for Christ International, Arrowhead Springs, San Bernardino, California 92403.

Life. "For God so loved the world, that He gave His only begotten Son, that whosoever believeth in Him should not perish, but have everlasting life" John 3:16.

"I am come that they might have life, and that they might have it more abundantly" John 10:10b.

2 *Man Is Sinful And Separated From God, Thus He Cannot Know And Experience God's Love And Plan For His Life.*

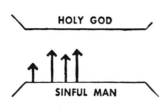

"For all have sinned and come short of the glory of God" Romans 3:23.

"For the wages of sin is death; but the gift of God is eternal life through Jesus Christ our Lord" Romans 6:23.

3 *Jesus Christ Is God's Only Provision For Man's Sin. Through Him You Can Know God's Love And Plan For Your Life.*

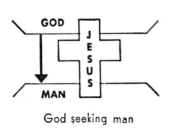

God seeking man

"But God commendeth His love toward us, in that, while we were yet sinners, Christ died for us" Romans 5:8.

"Jesus saith unto him, I am the way, the truth, and the life: no man cometh unto the Father, but by Me" John 14:6.

"For He hath made Him to be sin for us, who knew no sin; that we might be made the righteousness of God in Him" II Corinthians 5:21.

157

I skimmed through the first three laws, calling attention to the verses and the meaning of each diagram, because I knew they already believed the Gospel, but had never asked Jesus Christ into their lives. Then I said, "This fourth law is the one I want you to look at closely. It is:

4 We Must Receive Jesus Christ As Savior And Lord By Personal Invitation."

I continued by saying, "From this law you can see that it isn't enough to accept Christ as your Savior to forgive your past mistakes, you need to accept Christ as your SAVIOR and LORD. You need a Lord to guide your future. This diagram will show you what I mean. The circle

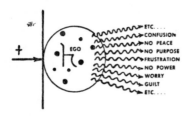

represents your life. The chair represents the control center of your will. The thing that makes us so different from animals is that God has given us a free will. We can do as we please. That is what the Ego means on the throne in the circle. It is the big "I." The dots represent big and little decisions of life that must be made: where will I work, whom will I marry, how will I treat my partner, what kind of friends will I have, and many other decisions. The problem with this life is that Christ is on the outside and Ego is making the decisions. As long as a person makes decisions based on 'What I want,' or 'What is good for me,' he will be filled with degrees of frustration, fear, confusion, no purpose, guilt, and many other problems.

"Now if a person is willing to receive Christ into his life as Lord and Savior, the result will be different. Christ will come into his life and take over the throne of his will.

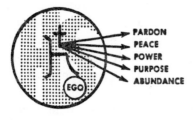

The first thing Christ does is pardon and cleanse *all* of his sins. That produces peace in his heart because when a person's sins are forgiven he no longer fears God. When Christ comes into his life he has a new source of power which enables him to fulfill his thrilling new purpose in life. Furthermore, Christ, through his Spirit, gives us a new abundance of life: new love, joy, and peace—which are man's basic needs."

I went on to say, "It really isn't hard to receive Christ into your life. John 1:12 says, 'But as many as received Him to them gave He power to become the sons of God, even to them that believe on His name.' In Revelation 3:20 the Lord Jesus said, 'Behold, I stand at the door, and knock: if any man hear My voice, and open the door, *I will* come in to him.' Receiving Christ is simply recognizing that you want him to come into your life to forgive your past and guide your future so you ask him by prayer to come in. By this act of your will you give yourself emotionally, mentally, and physically to Christ."

Then I said, "Now I want to ask you two something, Which of these circles represents your life right now?" I held the circles up so they could see them clearly.

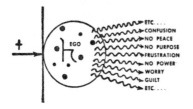

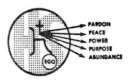

Within a few seconds they agreed that the first circle represented their lives. Then I asked, "Do you know any reason why you couldn't invite Christ into your lives right now?" Tom said, "I don't, it's just what I need." His wife said simply, "Me too." Right then these two young people prayed their first prayer. They weren't profound or long prayers; they simply admitted to God that they were sinners and asked the Lord Jesus to come into their lives as Lord and Savior.

In a moment of time they became "children of God, new creatures in Christ." The transformation isn't always so apparent as it was with them. After I gave them a few ideas on the assurance of salvation and on how to grow in their Christian life they left, holding hands.

A week later they were back. They were amazed at the change in their marriage. I asked, "What is the biggest change that you have noticed in yourselves?" They said, "The quick and complete return of our love for each other."

I have watched this couple for several months now. Whenever I see the tender and affectionate way they treat each other and recall the hatred and bitterness that existed between them before, I rejoice again that the Gospel of Jesus Christ is still the "power of God unto salvation to every one that believeth..." (Romans 1:16).

Before you close this book may I ask you a question? Which of the circles on page 159 represents your life?

If it's the first one, I would like to urge you to let Christ come into your life and introduce you to abundant living. He has the answer to every problem and difficult situation and will direct you in being "happy though married."

From the Private Library of
P. Craig Collins

58997

How to be happy though married
248.84 L183h   58997

LaHaye, Tim F.
Overton Memorial Library